The Least of All Possible Evils

The Least of All Possible Evils

Humanitarian Violence from Arendt to Gaza

EYAL WEIZMAN

VERSO

London • New York

The research for this book was supported by the European Research
Council (ERC) project Forensic Architecture and the Graham
Foundation for Advanced Studies in the Fine Arts

This edition first published by Verso 2011
© Eyal Weizman 2011

1 3 5 7 9 10 8 6 4 2

Verso
UK: 6 Meard Street, London W1F 0EG
US: 20 Jay Street, Suite 1010, Brooklyn, NY 11201
www.versobooks.com

Verso is the imprint of New Left Books

ISBN-13: 978-1-84467-647-7

British Library Cataloguing in Publication Data
A catalogue record for this book is available from the British Library

Library of Congress Cataloging-in-Publication Data
A catalog record for this book is available from the Library of Congress

Typeset in Garamond by Hewer Text UK Ltd, Edinburgh
Printed by the Tien Wah Press, Singapore

For TP and SP, who will know when they grow

Contents

Itzhak Ben Israel explains to Yotam Feldman his mathematical equation for the destruction of Hamas by eliminating (arresting or killing) its operatives. 'The Lab' 2011.

1

The Humanitarian Present

Having survived the butchery of a gruesome battle, Candide escapes the army and comes upon his long-time tutor Pangloss. The two decide to set out on a sea journey. A tempest wrecks their ship, killing almost all aboard. Pangloss and Candide are washed ashore in Lisbon upon a plank. 'Hardly do they set foot in the city . . . than they feel the earth tremble beneath them; a boiling sea rises in the port and shutters the vessels lying at anchor. Great sheets of flames and ash cover the streets and public squares; houses collapse, roofs topple on to foundations, and foundations are levelled in turn; thirty thousand inhabitants without regards to age or sex are crushed beneath the ruins.'[1] But master Pangloss, emerging from under a pile of the city's rubble – drawings of which later generations will regard as the 'first media representations of a distant catastrophe'[2] – argues that there is no effect without a cause. He explains to Candide that divine calculations, obscure to the human mind, mean that all that happened is 'for the very best'. For Pangloss, of course, all was always for the best in the best of all possible worlds. Voltaire's grotesque satirical adventure novel continues across seas and continents, witnessing the cruelties, violence and destruction of both the human and divine order: from war in Europe through storms and earthquakes to the colonialism of the eighteenth century in the Americas. Indeed across the Atlantic, our two protagonists observe how the Jesuits in Paraguay, claiming to have arrived there to help and redeem the indigenous peoples, actually abuse and enslave them.

Candide was written in the wake of the 1755 Lisbon earthquake, tsunami and fire, and in the middle of the Seven Years' War, which wreaked havoc across Europe and its American colonies. In the shadow of this catastrophe a new order of urban planning emerged in Lisbon, a gridded geometry that was later exported to the American colonies. The sequence of devastation, described above, prompted Voltaire to challenge and ridicule Leibnizian optimism and with it the concept of 'necessity,' which implies that destructive events somehow serve an invisible and mysterious purpose in a world in which the relationship between good and evil is always optimal. Leibniz himself had been buried two decades when the Lisbon earthquake struck, but it was he who had proposed the scheme of 'the best of all possible worlds' in order to reconcile all the apparent evils in the world – floods, starvations, wars, storms, tsunamis, epidemics, pandemics, earthquakes, fires and other phenomena we now like to refer to as 'emergencies' – with the idea of divine providence, which is necessarily omnipotent, omniscient and omnibenevolent – all-powerful, knowing, and good.[3] Leibniz's attempt to solve this age-old theological aporia involved a conception of God as an economist that managed the world by solving a minimum problem in the calculus of variations. Choosing for the optimum combination of good and evil involves a constant monitoring of the world, a task undertaken by examinining its smallest units – which Leibnitz called monads. These are substances that contain the imprint of all worldly relations, powers and effects. In a process resembling a 'divine forensics' God infers from these fragments what is happening everywhere in the universe. The examination is of course not about a crime, or other forms of imperfection, in the present or past – all things that do exist are necessarily the best possible things – but rather is the condition for choosing the best next possible world in the future.[4]

Divine examination, evaluation, calculation and choice operate thus within a complex economy in which good and bad could be transferred and exchanged. Because in this economy all bad things necessarily appear at their minimum possible level, the world as lived is always necessarily the best of all possible worlds. 'If a lesser evil is relatively good,' Leibniz reasoned, 'so a lesser good is relatively evil . . . to show that an architect could have done better is to find faults in his work.'[5]

If this description of the economy of divine government is already reminiscent of the logic of contemporary wars, with its own scales of risk and proportionality used to evaluate the desired and undesired consequences of military acts, it is hardly surprising to find in it an early reflection on the concept of 'collateral damage'. Earlier Christian theology has indeed already described all bad things that take place as 'the collateral effects of the good'. In this immanent order of human and divine life, the destructive result of floods are nothing but the collateral effect of necessary rain. In both their theological and military contexts, as Giorgio Agamben observed, the collateral effects are structural rather than accidental. It is through the collateral – flood or blood – that a government – divine or human – can demonstrate, indeed exercise, its power. [6]

Unlike the calculations of a God, seen by the philosophers and the theologians of the eighteenth century as a perfect mathematician who could undertake instantaneous calculations and immediatly arrive at a precise result, mere humans must of course guess, speculate and hedge their risks as they proceed towards the future as the blind leading the blind. It is for this reason that they ceaselessly seek to develop and perfect all sorts of technologies and techniques that might allow them to calculate the effects of violence and might harness its consequences. It is these techniques and technologies, apparatuses and spatial arrangements, that are at the heart of this book. Through them, Pangloss's Leibnizian scheme – or is it Leibniz's Panglossian scheme? – of the 'best of all possible worlds' re-emerges in the progressive tradition of liberalism. Here, in its secularized form, political rather than metaphysical, a similar structure of the argument sets up the sphere of morality as a set of calculations aimed to approximate the optimum proportion between common goods and necessary evils. [7] But as the general outlook of liberalism shifted from Voltaire's and indeed Jeremy Bentham's later focus on the 'greater good' and the responsibility of government to increase happiness to the greatest number of people, to the liberal canards of 'just wars', and their increasingly sophisticated technologies for minimizing the number of 'necessary' corpses, the search for 'the best of all possible worlds' started giving ground to the present neo-Panglossian pessimism of the 'least of all possible evils'.

This book engages with the problem of violence in its moderation and minimization, mostly with state violence that is managed according to a similar economy of calculations and justified as the least possible means. The fundamental point of this book is that the moderation of violence is part of the very logic of violence. Humanitarianism, human rights and international humanitarian law (IHL), when abused by state, supra-state and military action, have become the crucial means by which the economy of violence is calculated and managed. A close reading of a series of case studies will show how, at present, spatial organizations and physical instruments, technical standards, procedures and systems of monitoring – the complex humanitarian assemblage that philosopher Adi Ophir called 'moral technologies' – have become the means for exercising contemporary violence and for governing the displaced, the enemy and the unwanted.[8] The condition of collusion of these technologies of humanitarianism, human rights and humanitarian law with military and political powers is referred to in this book as 'the humanitarian present'. Within this present condition, all political oppositions are replaced by the elasticity of degrees, negotiations, proportions and balances.

It was media scholar Sharon Sliwinski who described the Lisbon disaster as 'the first modern mass media event to a distant catastrophe', with its illustrations allowing Europeans across political boundaries to share in the horror of the event. Sliwinski explained that part of what helped eighteenth-century Europe experience the horror of this earthquake were graphic representations of destroyed buildings. These included 'highly detailed records of the important buildings ruined by the disaster', adding up to the first 'patient and careful forensic survey of damages that circulated throughout the rest of Europe as evidence of the event.'[9]

The chapters that make this book have a similar forensic dimension. They focus on the built environment, on spatial technologies, on scenes of destruction and on their representation and dissemination in photography, film, models and drawings. Each chapter offers a narrative account of a recent or contemporary controversy brought into crisis around problems of space; and each of the chapters engages with questions of a practical nature: what are the technologies, spatial arrangements, artefacts and environments that shape the humanitarian present? How do they function and how were they were developed and transformed over time? Physical structures and spatial techniques are the small units of analysis that compose this investigation. The 'forensic analysis' of their characteristics is an attempt to tease out the political forces, cultural habits, forms of knowledge, skills and expertise that were folded into their organization and form. The investigation of spatial reality is accompanied by accounts of the characters that initiated, developed and participated in the making of these technologies or were caught within the complex force-fields of the emergencies in which they were employed. They involve humanitarians, refugee organizations, human rights lawyers and others specializing in the laws of war, military specialists and forensic investigators working for different organizations and in different areas worldwide. The scenes recounted were chosen because each one demonstrates a different way to inhabit the complex conditions of this humanitarian present.

Chapter 2 traces the way in which the recognition that humanitarian relief has the potential to become lethal to the people it came to serve – a reality registered in comparative statistics of epidemeology and mortality rates – structured debates around possible ways to conceive and organize humanitarian spaces. It also examines the process by which these spaces have gradually become instruments for governing the displaced. Chapter 3 analyzes the physical and procedural siege mechanisms applied by Israel in the Gaza Strip, which were governed by the standards of the 'humanitarian minimum'. They operated by calibrating the level of electric current, calories and other necessities to the minimum possible level in an attempt to govern people by reducing them to the limit of bare physical existence. In Chapter 4, scientific and probabilistic models are examined in the use of forensic methodologies – and in particular the emergent practice of 'forensic architecture,' which is employed in the analyzes of the rubble left by war. These are shown to be based on the same lethal technologies they came to monitor in the first case. The book's epilogue presents an archive of destroyed buildings in Gaza, produced by the Hamas-run Ministry of Public Works and Housing in the wake of Israel's attack in the winter of 2008–9.

This study of ruins ends a process of transformation that is unfolded in the course of the book: it begins with a reflection on the role of testimony in the reinvention of humanitarianism in the early 1970s and ends with a reflection on its being superseded by forensic science. The shift is more than one which the misanthropic gaze of forensics, as exercised by scientists and former military personnel, replaces the 'empathic' attention to the testimony of the people who suffered; it also mirrors the transformation of the focus in the field of humanitarianism and human rights from a form of independent engagement with the pains of this world in the 1970s and 1980s to a political and military force in the 1990s, and finally into a legalistic strategy in the 2000s.

In tracing the way these transformations are registered in the microphysics of different spaces and scenes, the chapters and our protagonists move through Ethiopia, Kosovo, Bosnia, Iraq, Darfur, and Afghanistan. But it is in relation to Israel's domination of the Gaza Strip that these reflections converge. Gaza – where the system of humanitarian government is now most brutally exercised – is the proper noun for the horror of our humanitarian present.

665

If, as a friend recently suggested, we ought to construct a monument to our present political culture as a homage to the principle of the 'lesser evil', it should be made in the form of the digits 6-6-5 built of concrete blocks, and installed like the Hollywood sign on hillsides or other high points overlooking city centres. This number, one less than the number of the beast – that of the devil and of total evil – might capture the essence of our humanitarian present obsessed with the calculations and calibrations that seek to moderate, ever so slightly, the evils that it has largely caused itself.

The principle of the lesser evil is often presented as a dilemma between two or more bad choices in situations where available options are, or seem to be, limited. The choice made justifies the pursuit of harmful actions that would be otherwise deemed unacceptable in the hope of averting even greater suffering. Sometimes the principle is presented as the optimal result of a general field of calculations that seeks to compare, measure and evaluate different bad consequences in relation to necessary acts, and then to minimize those consequences. Both aspects of the principle are understood as taking place within a closed system in which those posing the dilemma, the options available for choice, the factors to be calculated and the very parameters of calculation are unchallenged. Each calculation is undertaken anew, as if the previous accumulation of events has not taken place, and the future implications are out of bounds.

Those who seek to justify necessary evils as 'lesser' ones, especially when searching for a rationale to explain recent wars and military expeditions, like to appeal to the work of the fourth-century North African

philosopher–theologian St Augustine. Augustine's rejection of the principle of Manichaeism – a world divided into equally powerful good and evil
– meant that he no longer saw evil as the perfect mirror image of the
good; rather, in platonic terms, as a measure of its absence. Since evil,
unlike good, is not perfect and absolute, it is forever measured and cali-
brated on a differential scale of more and less, greater and lesser. Augustine
taught that it is not permissible to practise lesser evils, because to do so
violates the Pauline principle 'do no evil that good may come'. But – and
here lies its appeal – lesser evils might be tolerated when they are deemed
necessary and unavoidable, or when perpetrating an evil results in the
reduction of the overall amount of evil in the world. One of the examples
Augustine gives for such an economy of lesser and greater evils is a
robbery on a crossroads. It is to this crossroads that other theologists,
philosophers and political theorists will return, to this day, when discussing the dilemma. In Augustine's logic of pre-emption, it is better to kill the
would-be assailant before he kills an innocent traveller. A millennium later
and the armies of Western Christendom passed through this ethico-
theological needle-eye-sized loophole on their way to the catalogue of
pillage and destruction that constituted the crusades. More recently, Pope
Benedict XVI has appealed to the lesser evil principle in a decree permit-
ting the use of condoms in places inflicted with high rates of HIV. Similar
to the latter logic of contraception, some in the Vatican thought that
implicit support of the government of Silvio Berlusconi, albeit plagued by
sin, ridicule and corruption, might after all be considered as the lesser evil
in protecting Christian values. In cases such as these, the economy of the
lesser evil is always cited as a justification for breaching rigid rules and
entrenched dogma; indeed, it is often used by those in power as the
primary justification for the very notion of 'exception'. In fact, Augustine's
discourse of the lesser evil developed at a time when the church had
started to participate in the political government of its subjects and had
acquired considerable financial and military power. Through the ages, the
Christian church increasingly saw its task as keeping human evil to its
minimum level. It pastorally ruled over a vast and complex intrapersonal
economy of merits and faults – of sin, vice and virtue – operating according to specific rules of circulation and transfer, with procedures, analyzes,
calculations and tactics that allow the exercise of a specific interplay

between conflicting goods and degrees of evil. In his lectures on the origins of governmentality, Michel Foucault argued that, on the basis of this 'economical theology', the modern, secular form of governmental power has itself taken on the form of an economy.[10]

Lesser Evildoers

The theological origins of the lesser evil argument still cast a long shadow on the present. In fact the idiom has become so deeply ingrained, and is invoked in such a staggeringly diverse set of contexts – from individual situational ethics and international relations, to attempts to govern the economics of violence in the context of the 'war on terror' and the efforts of human rights and humanitarian activists to manoeuvre through the paradoxes of aid – that it seems to have altogether taken the place previously reserved for the term 'good'. Moreover, the very evocation of the 'good' seems to everywhere invoke the utopian tragedies of modernity, in which evil seemed lurking in a horrible manichaeistic inversion. If no hope is offered in the future, all that remains is to insure ourselves against the risks that it poses, to moderate and lessen the collateral effects of necessary acts, and tend to those who have suffered as a result.

In relation to the 'war on terror', the terms of the lesser evil were most clearly and prominently articulated by former human rights scholar and leader of Canada's Liberal Party Michael Ignatieff. In his book *The Lesser Evil*, Ignatieff suggested that in 'balancing liberty against security' liberal states establish mechanisms to regulate the breach of some human rights and legal norms, and allow their security services to engage in forms of extrajuridical violence – which he saw as lesser evils – in order to fend off or minimize potential greater evils, such as terror attacks on civilians of western states.[11] If governments need to violate rights in a terrorist emergency, this should be done, he thought, only as an exception and according to a process of adversarial scrutiny. 'Exceptions', Ignatieff states, 'do not destroy the rule but save it, provided that they are temporary, publicly justified, and deployed as a last resort.'[12] The lesser evil emerges here as a pragmatic compromise, a 'tolerated sin' that functions as the very justification for the notion of exception. State violence in this model takes part in a necro-economy in which various types of destructive measure are weighed in a utilitarian fashion, not only in relation to the damage they produce, but to the harm they purportedly prevent and even in relation to the more brutal measures they may help restrain. In this logic, the problem of contemporary state violence resembles indeed an all-too-human version of the mathematical minimum problem of the divine calculations previously mentioned, one tasked with determining the smallest level of violence necessary to avert the greatest harm. For the architects of contemporary war this balance is trapped between two poles: keeping violence at a low enough level to limit civilian suffering, and at a level high enough to bring a decisive end to the war and bring peace.[13]

More recent works by legal scholars and legal advisers to states and militaries have sought to extend the inherent elasticity of the system of legal exception proposed by Ignatieff into ways of rewriting the laws of armed conflict themselves.[14] Lesser evil arguments are now used to defend anything from targeted assassinations and mercy killings, house demolitions, deportation, torture,[15] to the use of (sometimes) non-lethal chemical weapons, the use of human shields, and even 'the intentional targeting of some civilians if it could save more innocent lives than they cost.'[16] In one of its more macabre moments it was suggested that the atomic bombings of Hiroshima might also be tolerated under the defence of the lesser evil. Faced with a humanitarian A-bomb, one might wonder what, in fact, might come under the definition of a greater evil. Perhaps it is time for the differential accounting of the lesser evil to replace the mechanical bureaucy of the 'banality of evil' as the idiom to describe the most extreme manifestations of violence. Indeed, it is through this use of the lesser evil that societies that see themselves as democratic can maintain regimes of occupation and neo-colonization.

Beyond state agents, those practitioners of lesser evils, as this book claims, must also include the members of independent nongovernmental organizations that make up the ecology of contemporary war and crisis zones. The lesser evil is the argument of the humanitarian agent that seeks military permission to provide medicines and aid in places where it is in fact the duty of the occupying military power to do so, thus saving the military limited resources. The lesser evil is often the justification of the military officer who attempts to administer life (and death) in an 'enlightened' manner; it is sometimes, too, the brief of the security contractor who introduces new and more efficient weapons and spatio-technological means of domination, and advertises them as 'humanitarian technology'. In these cases the logic of the lesser evil opens up a thick political field of participation bringing together otherwise opposing fields of action, to the extent that it might obscure the fundamental moral differences between these various groups. But, even according to the terms of an economy of losses and gains, the concept of the lesser evil risks becoming counterproductive: less brutal measures are also those that may be more easily naturalized, accepted and tolerated – and hence more frequently used, with the result that a greater evil may be reached cumulatively.

Such observations amongst other paradoxes are unpacked in one of the most powerful challenges to ideas such as Ignatieff's – Adi Ophir's philosophical essay *The Order of Evils*. In this book Ophir developed an ethical system that is similarly not grounded in a search for the 'good' but rather in minimizing the harms that he refers to as 'evils'. Ophir unpacks the systemic logic of an economy of violence – the possibility of a lesser means and the risk of more damage – but insists that questions of violence are forever unpredictable and will always escape the capacity to calculate them. Inherent in Ophir's insistence on the necessity of calculating is, he posits, the impossibility of doing so. The demands of his ethics are grounded in this impossibility.[17]

Pangloss's Law

The diffuse body of customs and conventions that make up *jus in bello*, the laws of war otherwise known as international humanitarian law (IHL), have since the end of the Cold War increasingly become the frame within which the calculation and application of military violence takes place. In recent decades IHL has also become an important part of global political culture. Debates about conflicts and occupations from Kosovo to Afghanistan to Iraq tend to use the terminology of IHL. The juridical categories of 'necessity' and 'proportionality' seem to be among the most popular terms employed in designing and monitoring state violence. This applies also to the antiwar movements: it is now not uncommon to see demonstrators carrying banners with slogans bearing references to these clauses in the law (as in the oft-invoked recrimination of 'war crimes') or to specific legal principles such as proportionality ('disproportional attack'). Those protesting in the name of the law must remember, though, that IHL does not seek to end wars but rather to 'regulate' and 'shape' the way militaries wage them; and that western militaries, increasingly bogged down by a raft of urban insurgencies in various global arenas, are also keen to change the way they fight wars and to minimize civilian casualties. Western militaries tend to believe that by moderating the violence they perpetrate, they might be able to govern populations more efficiently and even finally win over the hearts and minds that have continuously eluded them since the British Malayan counterinsergency and the Vietnam War.

Within the frame of international humanitarian law the clearest manifestation of the lesser evil principle is the principle of *proportionality*. This is, of course, embedded in almost every civil legal code. Different versions of it have been used to describe different types of balancing acts, most often in situations where some rights contradict others, or when individual rights are weighed against public interests, or against administrative or economic policies.[18] Within the context of IHL, however, proportionality is a moderating principle that seeks to constrain the use of force.[19] The principle was implicit in most international conventions on the use of force but was formally codified only in 1977, in Protocol I of the Geneva Conventions. The protocol's wording prohibits 'an attack which may be expected to cause incidental loss of civilian life, injury to civilians, damage to civilian objects, or a combination thereof, which would be *excessive* in relation to the concrete and direct military advantage anticipated' (my emphasis).[20] Proportionality thus demands the establishment of a 'proper relation' between 'unavoidable means' and 'necessary ends'. While considering the choice of military means, the principle calls for a balance to be established between military objectives and anticipated damage to civilian life and property. Proportionality is thus not about clear lines of prohibition but rather about calculating and determining balances and degrees. In incessantly calculating for the least of all means possible, it embodies something of Pangloss's principle.

The purpose of proportionality is not to strike a perfect balance, but rather to ensure that there is no excessive imbalance. Nevertheless it is about the 'too much' – but how much is too much? Although violence is in constant need of measurement, the principle of proportionality provides no scale, no formulas and no numerical thresholds. Instead, it demands assessment on a case-by-case basis, within parameters that are always relative, situational and immanent. It demands the estimation of aims, impacts and side effects, intended and unintended consequences – which is also to say, the measurement of lesser and greater evils, their exchange and sometimes even transfer – in an economy of a real or imaginary 'worst-case scenario' and in an attempt to keep the overall level of violence to the minimum necessary. By opening a field of equivalence, in which different forms of potential and actual violence, risk, and damage become exchangeable, proportionality approximates an algorithmic logic of computation – although, still, in practice, it is rarely computed.

Military lawyers and experts in international humanitarian law are the first to accept the fact that the predictions required for proportionality analysis are always contingent, immanent and prone to subjective interpretations. Contemporary military debates about IHL concern precisely the impossibility of bringing together in practice the legal demand that violence be measured, and the impossibility of doing so. Like the finance specialists who acknowledge the impossibility of prediction but do little else than calculate, the economists of violence are incessantly weighing their options and hedging their risks under the assumption of unpredictability and uncertainty. It is the very act of calculation – the very fact calculation took place – that justifies their action. Indeterminacy, the very principle that makes the economies of liberal capitalism generate profit, or burst after a sequence of failures, is also central to the conduct and potential outcomes of the contemporary wars.

But along with the growing capacity of technological means the incalculability of their consequences also grows. Some military lawyers think that indeterminacy will always work in their favour. Others, allergic to the idea of vagueness, see in technology an opportunity to dispel inherent uncertainties and incalculability. Daniel Reisner, former head of the International Law Division in the Israeli military, is of the latter kind. In a conversation he described to me the problems of calculating the economy of violence on the proportionality principle, and later his attempt tried to dispel something of the ethical/legal fog surrounding the question:

Proportionality is a complex logic with many variables – but how do you compare these? There is no choice but to ask the question, compare and calculate. Proportionality does not tell us what to include in the calculation, what is the equation and what is the exchange rate. Should a man of combatant age be counted as a civilian? If so, does he count for more or for less? How do you count women in relation to men? How do you count the death of children? Does one dead child equal one dead grownup, or does he equal five grownups? As a lawyer I need numbers to work with. I need thresholds in order to instruct the soldiers. Any number could become a useful benchmark. But when the ground of the law is shaking I am also unstable.

The legal definition of civilian does not, of course, involve any distinctions by gender and age; civilian life is civilian life and children are legally considered equal to adults. But lawyers' insistence on the fine details of a necro-economy, and the conversion rates between people of different genders and ages, is explained by the fact that proportionality has become a means to an end: measuring the public legitimacy of an act of violence. In this arena there is indeed a different meaning attached to the killing of children or women.

Lacking any other criterion for measurement, death ratio is one of the gruesome ways in which proportionality is calculated and managed in practice. It has its macabre side effects, too. In a 2002 meeting of a team of experts on law and military ethics, Reisner challenged his colleagues to an experiment. He asked each of them what ratio of 'collateral civilian death' – how many civilians killed – they considered to be legitimate in the context of a specific scenario that he recounted, of an armed militant about to be killed by the Israeli military. Each of his colleagues wrote down a number of civilian deaths they'd accept as legitimate under the principle of proportionality. The numbers were then counted and collated, and an average was calculated. It was 3.14 – very approximately the mathematical constant π whose value is the ratio of a circle's circumference relative to its diameter in Euclidean space. Another instance of calculation, while not referring directly to proportionality, embodies this grotesque logic of necro-economy in practice. In 2002, while still a general in the Israeli military, Itzhak Ben Israel, now a professor of physics at the

Tel Aviv University and chairman of Israel's space agency, was in charge of the 'weapons and technological infrastructure research and development directorate'. There he developed an equation based on systems theory in order to predict the necessary number of people the Israeli military must eliminate from a militant organization by arrest or targeted assassinations in order to defeat it. The formula was $Q=1-(q \ln q + 1/q \ln 1/q)$. In this equation, which seeks to apply the entropic behaviour of molecules in a gaseous state to military and political matters, Q stands for the probability that the organization will collapse and q is the percentage of militants you kill. To put it simply, if you kill (or neutralize in other ways) 20–25 per cent of the members of an organization – any organization – there is an 85 per cent likelihood that the confusion and knowledge loss generated will lead to its collapse. If you kill 50 per cent, the formula has it, the result converges on a 100 per cent probability that it will collapse.[21]

Proportionality's system of calculations approximates models applied in the insurance industry to assess risk. Risk analysis developed indeed as a means of determining the probabilities of bad things occurring, their potential for damage and their spatial or systemic distribution. For the military, risk is the means of determining the probability of destruction and injury to personnel and equipment and their potential severity. The conception of risk is central to the calculation of proportionality, especially when attempts to minimize civilian casualties is measured against potential harm to soldiers. The 'trade off' of risk means that reducing risk to the attacking military tends to increase the risk to civilians. One of the clearest examples for this 'risk transfer war' was NATO's bombing of Kosovo and Belgrade in 1999. This was mainly due to the decision to conduct high altitude aerial attacks that reduced the danger to NATO air force, but dramatically increased it for the civilians on the ground. The result – no combat fatalities among NATO forces compared with five hundred civilians killed by the bombardment – was understood by many international law scholars as an indication of a breach of the proportionality principle. This case also demonstrated that the balance expected in proportionality has a territorial dimension. Different calculations, formulas, balances and death ratios are deemed appropriate to state militaries in different zones of action and across different borders.[22]

Calculating Machines for the Reduction of Evil

Could IHL ever produce operational software that guides the behaviour of robotic weapons? Reisner has recently joined a group of software engineers and military officers in an effort to develop what he describes as 'mathematical tools to tackle the problems of proportionality, something akin to an automatic system for military ethics and international law handled by software.' He is aware of actual and potential opposition to this system, both within and outside the military. 'Initially these systems would help officers in decision-making in real-time situations, but in cases of automatic and robotic warfare, the calculations and decisions would be taken by the machines themselves, in conformity with the laws of war.' When confronted by a critique articulated on humanist grounds – to the effect that these weapons could not have 'human compassion' or the capacity for 'human judgement', he retorts by pointing to human propensity for cruelty and excess. He is convinced that his 'system would not only be as good as humans but rather better than them: cooler and more precise within the purview of a law-driven paradigm.'[23] Even in this chess game, the computer is expected to beat its programmer.

Reisner emphasized two of the advantages that might come with the computation of proportionality. First, thresholds could be numerically defined, and the ratio of acceptable civilian casualties to military deaths could be decided in advance, facilitating planning. Second, a computer system would be without 'the tendency for cruelty that some individuals have'. In this Reisner might have been thinking about research by the American scientist Ronald Arkin, a leader in the field of weaponized robotics who worked to develop and promote 'ethical' robotic warfare on similar grounds. Arkin also explains that robots have no joy in violence. They do not get angry, scared or panicked under fire – the states of mind in which excess might lead to war crimes – but most importantly they are expendable: they do not have to defend themselves at the risk of others. A robot would have no problem making the ultimate ethical choice and destroying itself. Arkin describes the ethical/legal algorithms that would govern the life and death of robots as something akin to a governor in a steam engine. Just as the governor shuts down the engine when it runs too hot, the 'ethical governor' would operate as an artificial stop-action, or self-destruct option, in the ethical/legal domain when a numerical threshold gets crossed or when rules of engagement and battlefield protocols are about to be breached.[24] In this argumentation the 'rational' self-sacrifice of the machine is understood as the perfect mirror image of the 'irrational' self-sacrifice of the suicide bomber. Furthermore, in situations such as Israel's occupation of Gaza where an increased number of robotic technologies are employed to police and control an increasingly famished population, the assumed higher ethical position of robotic and other high-technology killing emphasizes the growing distance between the post-human colonizer and the barely human colonized.

In contemporary warfare, however, robots could not be thought of as singular instruments but parts of a flexible and synergic network of heterogeneous components consisting of human, automatic and semi-automatic components. Because military action gradually becomes more systematic – in the sense that it is undertaken by a diffuse assemblage of sensors, automatic weapons, computers and optics together with human operators, overseers and regulators, it also becomes increasingly hard to isolate individual responsibility and liability in the traditional way. As one of the legal advisers for the International Committee of the Red Cross (ICRC) recently told me: 'within complex military systems, even when the most serious violations of IHL are committed, it is often not possible to identify individual war criminals. Where information is dispersed among multiple actors there may be no individual perpetrator to whom to attribute fault. Thus it is only deviant behaviour that could be prosecutable.' But deviant behaviour, rather than the systemic organized violence of the state military, is what the military itself might prosecute. 'Deviants who breach the military's own rules and undermine its discipline are a problem to the military. But it is the systemic violence and not these "rotten apples" that is the main cause of suffering inflicted on civilians.'[25] Therefore, from the perspective of a possible legal defence of a soldier accused of violating IHL, a situation might arise where it would be advisable to adopt a counterintuitive strategy: instead of arguing that he exhibited his humanity by doing less than he could have done or was ordered to do – the lesser evil justification – he might propose the opposite: that he actually did more or worse than what he was asked to. The breach of the techno-civilized logic of computation and calculations could thus be argued as madness itself.

An Ethical Governor

The analogy of the ethical governor is a revealing one. When enacted by state militaries as a self-imposed form of restraint, the 'minimizing' function of humanitarian law often coincides with other military objectives. As legal scholar David Kennedy suggested, 'humanitarian law becomes a blueprint for military efficiency: it regulates how the military would best achieve its objectives without unnecessary use of force.'[26] Containing the number of civilian casualties is often seen as a useful strategy. A high proportion of casualties might fuel rage or resistance in ways that hinder a military's ability to govern effectively. Adherence to the proportionality principle helps focus the power of limited means. Thus it is in its moderation, rather than in its unrestrained application of power, that state violence becomes effective. The calculations of proportionality as a technique of management and government – the management of violence and the government of populations – is undertaken by the powerful side 'on behalf' of those it subjugates. Moreover this power is grounded in the very ability to calculate, count, measure, balance and act on these calculations. Inversely, to make oneself ungovernable, one must make oneself incalculable, immeasurable, uncountable.

The current textbook for US counterinsurgency – the infamous Field Manual FM 3-24, drafted in 2005 under the command of General David Petraeus, and used in Baghdad and Afghanistan by him and Stanley McChrystal to implement the surges – is perhaps the best example of a collusion of interests between international humanitarian law and human rights principles on the one hand, and the demands of military efficiency on the other. Sarah Sewall, then director of Harvard University's Carr Center for Human Rights, co-sponsored and co-organized the military 'doctrine revision workshop' for the purpose of drafting this manual and was one of its most enthusiastic supporters.[27] In her introduction to the Chicago University Press version of the manual, Sewall announced it as the product of an 'unprecedented collaboration [between] a human rights center partnered with the armed forces'. Military actions that cause civilian deaths are, she stated, 'not only morally wrong but tactically self-defeating'.[28] 'A short-term focus on minimizing risks to counterinsurgent forces', she writes, 'can ironically increase the risks to the larger campaign, including the longer-term vulnerability of US forces.' In this way, the manual allowed humanitarian law and human rights principles to become tools in the hands of an occupying military in trying to win over civilian populations – to become a technique of government. Before he was relieved of his duties by President Obama, General Stanley McChrystal was one of the manual's most devoted followers and, as chief of NATO forces in Afghanistan, its implementing arm. In his initial address to the US military in Afghanistan, McChrystal explained how adherence to mitigating principles of the law would be militarily effective: 'Our strategy cannot be focused on seizing terrain or destroying insurgent forces; our objective must be the population . . . we run the risk of strategic defeat by pursuing tactical wins that cause civilian casualties or unnecessary collateral damage.'[29] The new kind of soldier he thought must be a social worker, an urban planner, anthropologist and psychologist. It was such comments that prompted a prominent military historian to describe contemporary war as 'social work with guns'.[30] These processes are applicable in so far as military violence is understood as intervention in, rather than a replacement of, politics. Contemporary militaries see urbanized environments as complex social fields saturated by pre-existing conflicts. It is the very nature of urban areas – with their tendencies to density, congestion, diversities and heterogeneity – to foster conflicts in which different social, national or ethnic groups are at permanent conflict with each other. When military violence is introduced into a field that is already saturated with violence, it seeks to extenuate and unleash the potential conflicts already latent within the city in political, sectarian or communitarian form. The military would then sometimes refer to aerial bombing as the 'injection of kinetic energy into the fabric of social relations'.

Indeed, when using the population's well-being as part of a military calculus, we must be aware of the stick that hides behind any carrot. Any utilitarian use of humanitarian and human rights principles must acknowledge the possibility of its inverse and the speed by which such inversion could occur. If protecting civilians is used as a way of convincing people to comply with military government, at other times inflicting pain on them might usefully achieve the same ends – such as in situations when militaries want to force civilians to exert political pressure on their govern-ments or militants for example. According to this logic, harming civilians is not only a 'regrettable' collateral product of military counterinsurgency, but part of an overall logic of this form of military government – as seen, infamously in Fallujah in 2004, in Lebanon in 2006 and Gaza in 2008–9, when this pressure was thought to weaken resistance by hurting its civilian base. Increasing the harm to civilians can then be undertaken and moni-tored using the same tools conceived to reduce it.

War of the Mad

Military violence, then, endeavours not only to bring death and destruc-tion to its intended targets but also to communicate with its survivors – those that remain, those not killed. The laws of war have become one of the ways in which military violence is interpreted by those who experience it, as well as by global bystanders. It could thus be said to have a pedagogi-cal pretension. It is a violence that should not only convince but also manufacture the possibility for conviction. In contemporary war, the principle of proportionality has become the main translator of the relation between violence, law and its political meaning.

The communicative dimension of military threats can function only if gaps are maintained between the possible destruction that an army is able to inflict and the actual destruction that it does inflict. It is through the constant demonstration of the existence and size of this gap that the mili-tary communicates with the people it fights and occupies. Sometimes the gap opens wide, such as when the military governs the territories it occu-pies – its violence in a state of potential, existing as a set of threats and possibilities that are not, for the time being, actualized. In a state of war the gap closes – but rarely does it do so completely. Even in the most brutal of wars, something of the gap still exists as the stronger side restrains and moderates its full destructive capacity. Restraint is also what allows for the possibility of further escalation, an invitation for those people receiving violence to make their own cost-benefit calculation and opt for consent. A degree of restraint is thus part of the logic of almost every military operation: however bad military attacks may appear to be, they can always get worse. The gap is measured also against 'the potentiality of the worst' – an outburst of performative violence without rules, limits, proportion or measures – which has to be demonstrated from time to time. This necessarily creates a precedent against which all other bad events are understood and measured. With the initial recording of 'the worst', its reappearance, as Hannah Arendt commented, becomes ever more likely.[31]

The gap thus communicates the potential for destruction without the need for further violence. When the gap between the possible and the actual application of force closes completely, violence loses its function as a language. War becomes total war – a form of violence stripped of semiotics, in which the enemy is expelled, killed or completely reconstructed as a subject. Degrees in the level of violence are precisely what makes war less than total. Game theory, as applied by military think tanks since the early Cold War days of RAND, is conceived to simulate the enemy's responses, and help manage the gap between actual and potential violence. This practical form of military restraint is now often presented as the adherence to the laws of war.

While symmetric interstate warfare assumes a language that is well understood by both parties, and a rational basis for calculating the losses and profits of war, colonial violence presupposes that the language itself has to be constructed. Colonial wars have often been total wars, because the people colonized were not perceived to share the same humanity as the colonizers, and were therefore not seen as a party capable of rational behaviour and discourse. These wars are not about an enemy that has to be convinced but about an irrational people that has to be either reconstructed or killed. In these pedagogical wars, it is the *disproportional* violence of the madmen that is reserved. If proportionality stands for the ethical, rational aspect of war, in which the economy of balances functions well, then breaking this economy is intended as a message of a different order and magnitude.[32] 'We will wield disproportionate power against every village from which shots are fired on Israel, and cause immense damage and destruction . . . This is not a suggestion. This is a plan that has already been authorized.'[33] Similar statements by members of the Israeli security establishment and politicians, including the prime minister, proliferated in the aftermath of the 2006 Lebanon War with Hezbollah, and in anticipation of the 2008 invasion of Gaza where such violence was actualized. Disproportionality – the breaking of the elastic economy that balances goods and evils – is violence in excess of the law, and one that is directed at the law. Disproportional violence is also the violence of the weak, the governed, those who cannot calculate and are outside the economy of calculations. This violence is disproportional because it cannot be measured and because, ultimately, having its justice not reflected in existing law, comes to restructure its basis altogether.

Bulls and Spiders

Behind the present use of the term 'lesser evil' is a rich history and various intellectual trajectories. What may otherwise seem to be a perennial problem, endemic to ethics and political practice, a dilemma that recurs in different moments in time in the same shape and form, might in fact reveal something peculiar about each moment and situation. The various political, theological and philosophical uses of the lesser evil idiom may suggest that it meant different things to different people in different periods and situations. Every political tradition and form of political practice developed its own ways of engaging with the lesser evil argument – and much has subsequently been lost in translation. For example, unlike the tradition of liberal ethics that would invoke him centuries later, Augustine was never content with lesser evils. Indeed, a significant aspect of the idea of the lesser evil has been lost in its process of secularization from early Christian theology into the utilitarian foundations of liberal ethics. For the original Christian toleration of the lesser evil was understood in relation to the telos of redemption that is ultimately in excess of all calculations. For Augustine, the name for this state beyond calculations was 'the kingdom of heaven'. In contrast to the teachings of the Christian theologians that they invoked, and locked within a perpetual economy of immanence, liberal ethics can be interpreted as a drive for the 'optimization' of a system of government. But what is the sense in optimizing those regimes when they perpetuate intolerable injustice? Even those of us without much use for a 'kingdom of heaven' and without much patience for the systems of pastoral government that should guide us to it, can still see in

Augustine's argument an important challenge: how to engage in political practice within the complex existing force-fields of the present in a way that also aims to break away from them? This challenge is particularly acute for those who operate within or in relation to situations they deem intolerable and want to fundamentally change rather than reform. The practices of human rights could be used as effective tools against close societies and tyrannies, and were indeed often used in struggles that ended up replacing those regimes, they lend themselves easily for manipulation in the context of liberal democracies.

At different times, Marx, Lenin, Kautski, Luxemburg, Trotsky and Gramsci grappled with the problem of the lesser evil in fighting for gains here and now, while also fighting for a different and better world on the other. At various points they advocated struggles for immediate gains – for example, proposing trade unions, whose function was to win a better deal for workers in an exploitative system. None of them, however, thought that trade unions were all that was possible, and none was satisfied with simply winning a better deal within an existing system. Unlike the revolutionary and militant communists who protested the drift towards a timid, reformist politics of choosing the lesser evil and of making compromises with capital, Marx thought that winning a ten-hour day was a considerable victory for the English proletariat. Marx's argument shifted the attention from the ten hours of work to the fourteen hours of non-work time. These he thought provided the opportunity to build an organizational platform, as well as the consciousness and experience needed to take over the means of production.

To show that it is futile to object to all lesser evil compromises on principle, we could even enlist Lenin himself. In his attempt to explain the Treaty of Brest–Litovsk that lead to Soviet Russia's exit from World War I in 1918 after making an agreement with the western powers, Lenin returned to a scene of a road robbery described by Augustine. 'To reject compromises "on principle", to reject the permissibility of compromises in general, no matter of what kind', said Lenin, 'is childishness . . . One must be able to analyze the situation and the concrete conditions of each compromise, or of each variety of compromise. One must learn to distinguish between a man who has given up his money and firearms to bandits so as to lessen the evil they can do and to facilitate their capture and execution, and a man who gives his money and firearms to bandits so as to share in the loot.'[34] The deliberation of a political thought-practice must indeed insist on uncovering the force-field within which each of the dilemmas of the lesser evil exists, seeking to identify more extended and intricate political connections; looking further into the future, it should insist on political goals and the means of their achievement.

At one end of the spectrum, in which the lesser evil argument occupies the middle ground, stand those who believe that every possible gain at present is insignificant in light of the essentially compromised state of the world. Part of the structure of this argument is found the principle of the *politique du pire* – the politics of making things worse. This line of thought believes in the redemptive potential of misery – or in its theological-political incarnation as *dolorism*: pain as a spiritual experience that allows people to see more clearly. Every form of improvement is necessarily seen as the normalization of exploitation or the pacification of injustice. Opting for the worst is, therefore, an attempt to undermine the field of alternatives of a pre-given choice and overcome its terms.

But are the horrific spectacles of greater evils preferable to the incremental damage of lesser ones? Is the choice only between squabbling with power about the correct measure of its violence, helping to calibrate it and tend to its wounded, or on the other hand a call for its amplification in order to 'expose its contradictions' (contradictions seem only to sustain power's march) to shock a complacent population into rising up? Between refusal and tactical embrace the difficulty of the dilemma of the lesser evil is equally in practising and in avoiding it. The Greeks thought of the dilemma as one of the elements of tragedy. Each of the options that a tragic hero faces necessarily leads to different forms of horrific suffering: the dilemma was presented as a choice between the two horns of an angry bull. But the options must not only be about which of the horns to choose. Robert Pirsig has suggested several ways to subvert this complicity of the opposites: one can 'refuse to enter the arena', 'throw sand in the bull's eyes', or 'sing the bull to sleep'.[35]

The contemporary forms of power unpacked in this book are no longer so singular and unified. Rather than a bull, they may appear to take on the shape of a multiplicity, a diffuse field of forces simultaneously aggressive and benign. It is a form of power that not only charges forward;

it surrounds, immerses and embeds. Political activists must constantly invent new forms of struggle that are recognisant of this paradigm of power, but which also evade and subvert its embrace, attempt to *rewire* its webs in order to escape its calculation. The characters that inhabit the chapters of this book have stepped right into the thick of this web of forces: their movement through them offer valuable examples and lessons. Some paths must be avoided at all costs; others illuminate possible courses of action within the intricate workings of the humanitarian present.

Korem Relief Centre, Photo: MSF, 1985, Courtesy of MSF-France Archive Collection.

2

Arendt in Ethiopia

If we look at the techniques of totalitarian government, it is obvious that the argument of 'the lesser evil' . . . is one of the mechanisms built into the machinery of terror and criminality. Acceptance of lesser evils is consciously used in conditioning the government officials as well as the population at large to the acceptance of evil as such . . . Politically, the weakness of the argument has always been that those who choose the lesser evil forget very quickly that they chose evil.[1]

Hannah Arendt, 1964

There is probably a limit beyond which everything can backfire, a kind of threshold beyond which the meaning of any position is turned on its head. But I think that we can overcome this contradiction, at least in part, by upholding a vision of humanitarianism as the policy of the lesser evil . . . So accepting the policy of the lesser evil seems to me to be one way to live with the contradiction [of humanitarianism] without completely becoming a victim of it.[2]

Rony Brauman, 2006

The Ethiopian famine of the mid 1980s brought the idea of humanitarianism into crisis. This complex and large-scale episode drew militaries and militias, people displaced by famine and war, aid workers from dozens of organizations, government representatives, the UN, journalists and human rights advocates into an entangled zone of humanitarian management. Not only was this zone the place where relief was provided; it was

the frame through which the story of the famine was told and disseminated. Allegations concerning the abuse of aid, fiercely argued at the time,
still resonate in the media, with new revelations regarding the role that
was played by the present government of Ethiopia linking the humanitarian politics of the Cold War with the humanitarian strategy of the war
on terror.[3]

The controversy surrounding the Ethiopian crisis of the 1980s made
apparent the potential for abuse in humanitarianism, the fact that it can
aggravate the suffering of the people it is intended to help; it also heralded
a new possibility: the withdrawal of aid workers from desperate but
potentially compromising situations. This transformative episode is here
a starting point for an investigation into the problems and conflicts within
the field of humanitarianism in recent decades.

This chapter is based on a series of interviews with Rony Brauman,
former president of Doctors Without Borders (Médecins Sans Frontières,
or MSF) and now the director of its research think tank. It tells his story
against the background of the changing operational modes of independent humanitarianism throughout the wars and calamities of the past three
decades. It also aims to explain and bridge the gap in the use of the idiom
of the 'lesser evil', differently articulated in the two quotes above, and
brings together across different decades and continents the main protagonists of this chapter: Rony Brauman and Hannah Arendt.

In the autumn of 1984, the French writer Pascal Bruckner gave a copy of
Hannah Arendt's *Eichmann in Jerusalem* to the president of MSF, Rony
Brauman. Bruckner had just published the polemics that would irrevoca-
bly sever his ties with the left, in which he accused Western intellectuals
of uncritical support of 'totalitarian regimes disguised as utopian liberation movements in the "promised land" of the third world.'[4] Brauman
was then preparing to leave for northern Ethiopia, where MSF had been
involved in famine relief since April that year. Its medical team was based
in a relief camp near the small town of Korem, in the highland plateau
that formed the borderlands between the provinces of Wollo and Tigray,
where the Ethiopian military was engaged in fighting a brutal counterinsurgency against the Marxist–Leninist Tigrayan People's Liberation Front
(TPLF). Incidentally, it was close to Lake Ashenge where, on 3 April

1936, thousands of soldiers of the Ethiopian Empire were killed with poisonous mustard gas fired by Italian colonial forces.

Even before his departure for Korem, Brauman suspected that the promise of aid was being used by the Ethiopian regime to lure the inhabitants of the rebel zones into places from where they would be forcefully transferred. 'We were attracting people like bait in a trap. Local people knew they should never trust this violent, dictatorial government, but as aid workers were permanently dwelling in these so-called relief camps, [people] gained confidence and walked to them.'[5] Bruckner thought that Arendt's book might shed light on Brauman's predicament. Brauman took the book with him to Ethiopia and, having read it, discussed it one evening with colleagues in the mission's quarters.

> When I read *Eichmann in Jerusalem* with the Ethiopian issue in mind, I understood the terms of our problem. Through Arendt I discovered the hard notion of totalitarianism. I identified the Ethiopian regime with Nazi totalitarianism, and myself somewhere in between the Jewish councils and Eichmann. We wanted the good of the people we were there to help, we wanted to relieve their suffering . . . but we were supporting the deportation in various aspects.[6]

Brauman used the Jewish councils as an analogy because they collaborated with the Nazis by assisting in policies of population transfer. He acknowledged the crucial difference with his predicament in that the humanitarians have had no 'guns pointed to their heads' while making these choices.[7] However, against the totalitarian order imposed by Mengistu's red terror, the only reasonable response, he thought, was disorder and disobedience. With this, the imaginary geography of humanitarianism seems to have taken a giant leap in mapping the horrors of European history onto the Cold War frontiers in Africa and the ethnic fissures that precipitated it, but this imaginary geography was also very present in the mind-set of many Europeans who in preceding years transformed the practice of humanitarian aid.

The famine was, however, real enough.[8] Accounts of it tend to either foreground environmental conditions – thereby playing down its human causes – or political and military ones, thereby failing to account for the way in which environmental degradation led to a prolonged series of

Failed crops in Welo (left), and Korem Relief Centre (right), Ethiopia 1984.
Stills from: 'MSF: Ethiopia 1984', courtesy of MSF-France Archive Collection.

conflicts along the slowly desertifying belt of the Sahel. In this arid zone, which runs across Africa, connecting northern Ethiopia in the east with Darfur and Chad, then moving through Niger, Mali and on to Mauritania on the west coast, political and environmental conditions were entangled.

Food and water are scarce along this belt, accounting for a series of conflicts that aggravated the situation and lead on some occasions for famine to break out. As sudden as the famine of the 1980s might have appeared from an international perspective, it was in fact the culmination of a drought cycle that extended back into the '60s. It was the selfsame sequence that caused the farmers' revolts and marches on the cities that helped bring about the end of Emperor Haile Selassie's rule in September 1974.

Whether caused by war, drought or pests, famine is often understood in terms that are moral, political and theological, and it can lead to, or play a role in, political revolts. Upon seizing power in 1974, Colonel Mengistu Haile Mariam embarked upon the reshaping of Ethiopian society in the image of his patron, the USSR, nationalizing farmlands and abolishing the remnant of the pervasive feudal land-tenure system. In the early 1980s environmental and political conditions deteriorated simultaneously. Plans for the demographic reorganization of the countryside were implemented according to East German and Cuban designs for collective 'farm-clusters'

in the south-west of the country, in areas far away from the front and under government control. Infrastructure was extremely rudimentary and there were no farm facilities. However, the main reason that most people did not want to move was because of ethnic and linguistic differences. In the winter of 1984 the insurgency of the TPLF and the government's counterinsurgency led to the destruction of pastures, crops and grain stores. The area of severe famine corresponded with major military clashes, shifting with the war zone from Eritrea to Tigray and Welo. International agencies started arriving in the spring of 1984; among the first of them was MSF. Aid was provided in relief and distribution centres whose locations were determined by the Ethiopian government. Tens of thousands of weak and malnourished nomads and farmers walked to these centres in search of food. Brigitte Vasset, the director of operations, had to undertake a rapid evaluation in order to prioritize treatment in the small MSF clinic. 'Dominique, the nurse, and I felt like executioners. When people were admitted to the shelters, at least they had something to eat. Since there were always people arriving, we had to move the people who were doing better out of the shelters to make room. I remember measuring the circumference of people's arms. The adults whose arms I couldn't get my fingers around, they went outside; those whose arms were smaller, they went inside.'[9] Regardless of the condition of the people, when transport was available, the military rounded them up at gunpoint and moved them south. Some of these population transfers were made on buses and trucks

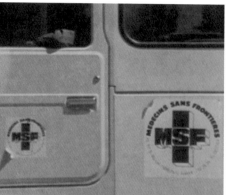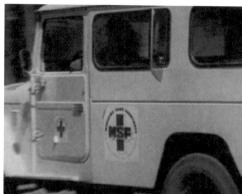

Korem, stills from: 'MSF: Ethiopia 1984', courtesy of MSF-France Archive Collection.

seized by the government from humanitarian organizations. Between 50,000 and 100,000 people died on the way or on arrival at the rudimentary and malaria-stricken settlements in the south.

The relief centre at Korem gradually developed into a central node for a number of systems. It was one of several food distribution and medical relief centres in the international aid effort. It had also grown into a hub for the ever-growing interest of the international media in the Ethiopian famine and became the lens through which the world observed what was happening. Most journalists were staying there, so it became the site where public information about the famine was produced and from where it was disseminated. Crucially, for the Ethiopian government, it also functioned as one of the largest centres for population concentration in a counterinsurgency effort that relied on transfer.

Aid was of course used as a strategy by all sides in this conflict. Some aid organizations – such as War on Want, run by then British Member of Parliament George Galloway – had a strong political affiliation with the rebels and established supply bases in neighbouring Sudan.[10] Food shipments from other organizations such as Oxfam were also handed to the TPLF, whose former leader, Meles Zenawi, is now Ethiopia's prime minister. The TPLF was supposed to deliver the shipments to starving peasants in Tigray. However, it is now alleged that the TPLF, like all the other participants in the conflict, used the sale of aid to purchase weapons.

Brauman felt that the humanitarian intervention worsened the situation for those that needed aid. It facilitated the implementation of the population transfer program. It was thus not just famine but, crucially, the famine-relief effort, sponsored by burgeoning public donations, that aggravated the situation. In an MSF board meeting in March 1985, Brauman explained that 'in Ethiopia we have realized that aid can kill. Through deportation financed by international aid. The more aid was coming into Ethiopia, the more people were dying. Although [the donors] believe they supported Ethiopia, in fact their money was used for purposes which were killing people – which were lethal.'[11]

Brauman goes on to describe how an ethical dilemma 'emerged between speaking out at the risk of being kicked out by the government, and continuing silently on the ground, at the risk of being accomplices to a crime'. This was not, he stressed, a choice between 'a political and a neutral position – as the neutral one was already inscribed in the political status quo – but between two political positions: one active, and the other by default.' Brauman alluded to Arendt's idea of withdrawal and refusal: 'If we accept that aid could be used against the people it is meant to assist, we must accept the possibility that in certain cases abstention or withdrawal may be preferable to action.'[12]

Between January and October 1985, Brauman gave several confrontational interviews, threatening to withdraw MSF from Ethiopia if the deportations didn't stop. The Ethiopian government explained that its

Aid airdrops in Ethiopia 1984. Still from Dangerous Pity, *Rony Brauman and François Margolin, 1996.*

demographic policies – moving people into safer and more fertile lands in the south of the country – were sovereign acts in a state of emergency caused by the famine, and indeed the lesser evil option given the scale of the hunger and the threats of future famines. The government also pointed out that during the Ethiopian famine of 1973 Haile Selassie had tried to resettle people from the northern provinces, and that in the early 1980s Soviet scientists had determined that the famines were aggravated by the overpopulation of the northern highlands, and that in order to manage the scarcity of food, bold solutions of social engineering such as population transfer were necessary.[13]

The mutual recriminations escalated throughout 1985. On 24 October, Ethiopia's Minister for Relief and Rehabilitation Dawit Wolde Giorgis announced,

> in view of the politically motivated false allegations made by [Brauman] and his refusal to follow norms and procedures . . . we are obliged to discontinue the services of Médecins Sans Frontières – France . . . MSF is one of the smallest of the fifty-seven private charity organizations in Ethiopia and has made a useful but marginal contribution to the overall gigantic national and international relief efforts . . . As a result MSF has always sought to make its presence felt by making more noise than miracles.

Later, drawing attention to what it described as MSF's 'neo-colonial attitude,' he added: 'Rony Brauman's little Tarzans have the biggest mouths
and they do the least . . . we are showing them the door and they should
walk right through it'.[14] In the meantime, after repeated clashes with other
NGOs – in particular with representatives of Oxfam and Concern – the
French ambassador to Ethiopia and Brauman almost came to blows after a
press conference in Addis Ababa in which the ambassador yelled at
Brauman, 'You are not worthy of being French . . . you are less than nothing', to which Brauman retorted, 'You would be a Pétainist under Pétain
and Gaullist under de Gaulle . . . I've got absolute contempt for you – fuck
you.' In a combative press conference after the MSF teams landed in
France, Brauman returned to his preoccupation: 'We can no longer say, as
some did after the Second World War, regarding the incredible passivity of
Europeans when they were confronted with the deportations: "We didn't
know!" '[15] And so, ideas regarding colonialism and postcolonialism, hunger
and repressive government, French collaboration and the Holocaust were all
clashing and bubbling together in unpredictable fashion. What a fine mess!

On Omelettes and Eggs

In Arendt's ethical philosophy, her argument against the 'lesser evil' was
perhaps the most controversial. It came to define how well-meaning citizens might be made to collaborate with totalitarian regimes. Arendt's

account of the forced collaboration of the Jewish councils with the Nazis sought to frame the extreme limit of the problem, suggesting that by opting at each stage for the lesser evil of trying to mitigate Nazi horrors – delivering named lists to the occupiers, selecting people for deportation, and even rounding them up, acts undertaken 'to avoid panic,' 'to minimize suffering' or 'for the larger good' – the *Judenräte* were made to work for the destruction of their own people. Arendt followed Raul Hilberg's well-known description of the councils as 'a self-destructive machine',[16] intending to show that at every occasion where the persecuted did not comply, failed to organize according to orders, did set up councils and did not attempt to moderate Nazi policies, their chances of survival, although slim, were still greater. Against all those who wanted to make things better from within (Arendt herself managed to leave), against all acts of collaboration, especially those undertaken for the sake of the moderation of harm, against the argument that the lesser evil of collaboration with brutal regimes is acceptable if it might mitigate, prevent or divert greater evils, she called for individual disobedience and collective disorder. When nothing else was possible, to do nothing was the last effective form of resistance, disorder was preferable to order, and the practical consequences of a refusal to cooperate were nearly always better than collaboration.[17] This seems to have been Brauman's motivation in pushing for withdrawal.

Brauman's interest in Arendt's account of the Eichmann trial led him, a decade later, to join the Israeli filmmaker Eyal Sivan in making the *The Specialist*, a film that followed the structure of Arendt's book in investigating the trial of Adolf Eichmann. In a book accompanying their film, they reiterated Arendt's position regarding the lesser evil: 'at the moment the Jewish councils became an instrument in the hands of the Nazis . . . the politics of the lesser evil became a way to hide the worst.'[18] Brauman later explained the lines of similarity between the councils and the humanitarians: 'in the case of Ethiopia, the aims of the NGOs and those of the totalitarians morphed into one another.'[19]

The Politics of Compassion

Arendt's work on totalitarianism was among the most important contributions to a discourse-practice that came to be known in the later years of the Cold War as 'anti-totalitarianism'. It has helped generate a multifaceted political shift within the left, largely promoted by post-1968 'Western radicals' who turned the focus of their political engagement to combating left-totalitarian regimes across the 'second' and 'third' worlds. For these former Marxists the 'general contradiction' was no longer between labour and capital but between democracy and totalitarianism. In this schema, an emphasis on the passive quasi-religious dialectics of victims and perpetrators replaced the active revolutionary designation of proletariat and bourgeoisie.

It was a transformation in which the Maoists of the late 1960s played an important role. The European Maoists were different from the other Marxist–Leninist factions in France in May 1968. Following what they mistakenly perceived to be the stakes in Mao's anti-establishment call of the Cultural Revolution, members of the Gauche Proletarienne (GP) led the revolt against all institutions of authority, including the French Communist Party (PCF). 'I come from a radical background', Brauman recalled. 'I was a Maoist belonging to the toughest Maoist group in France, the GP, and we were rallying in Paris to support and defend the Khmer Rouge, all through the 1970s, but when I saw that the first step they had taken was to empty the city of its population, it was my breaking point, and by the late 1970s I clearly became an anti-Communist . . . communism was not only impractical but in fact dangerous. Communism creates famine like clouds bring rain.'[20] The militancy of the former radicals persisted, but changed orientation. Their anti-authoritarianism shifted easily to anti-totalitarianism. In the late 1970s, the exposure of the Khmer Rouge's massacres in the name of a rural utopia coincided with the publication of Aleksandr Solzhenitsyn's *The Gulag Archipelago*. These, each in its own way, led to the distancing of many on the European left from Soviet bloc communism.

Many of these young activists and writers replaced an abstract concept of political 'justice' with an emotive idea of 'compassion', a revolutionary politics with one whose finite and practical goals are the relief of suffering in those regions of the world where it is most visible. The culture of immediate and direct action was easily transferred to the humanitarian culture of emergency.

Bernard-Henri Lévy, one of the most vocal members of what are called in France the 'new philosophers', summed up what they perceived as the most important choice: 'it was better to agree on Evil than on the Good, and once we agreed on what is Evil, [political practice] had to figure out how to lessen it . . . and make the world a little more liveable for the greatest number of people, and that we should not, therefore, make concessions about little things: life, rights here and now, human rights'.[21] Since 'evil' seemed to be lurking behind every attempt at political transformation and any liberation struggle, they believed that the destiny of the West was to fight that evil whose traces could be found, paradoxically, in any project predicated on an articulation of the idea of the totalitarian or egalitarian 'good'. The notion that the *nouveaux* polemicists espoused was fixed not on what we must do, but on what we must never again permit to be done. It was a transformation encapsulated by Judith Shklar's term 'the liberalism of fear',[22] in which the spectre of the worst – the replacement of law by totalitarian command – shaped the politics of the present. When utopia seems dangerous, what remains is only the preemptive management of this risk. The politics of the lesser evil was concerned with identifying situations considered to be intolerable, and with organizing the technology and means for interventions to stop or alleviate suffering. The globalization of compassion meant a view of humanity based on the figure of the victim. This compassion found its infrastructure in humanitarian organizations.

Paradoxically, the 'lesser evil' argument came to mean different and sometimes seemingly contradictory things. On the one hand, antitotalitarians acknowledged that Western-style liberal democracy was not a utopian ideal. In their view, it was close to Churchill's sardonic description of the comparative merits of democracy shortly after the end of World War II – 'the worst form of government except all those other forms that have been tried from time to time' – tolerable merely as a 'lesser evil'. Indeed, for anti-totalitarians, the looming spectre of totalitarianism led to the constant weighing of the injustices of liberal 'disorder' as 'the best of all possible worlds', when set against the worse evils of totalitarian tyranny. On the other hand, the same people vigorously advocated a stance against lesser-evil compromise and collaboration with regimes defined as totalitarian. Totalitarianism gave liberals the opportunity to fashion themselves as militant and radical. There were many before Dick Cheney to have said, 'We don't negotiate with evil, we defeat it.'

Reading Arendt on Eichmann, then, may indeed have been an eye-opener for Brauman, but it reflected humanitarianism's already deeply entrenched obsession with totalitarianism, Nazism being its paradigmatic example. With its abstract designations of 'good' and 'evil', the Holocaust has become for humanitarians the crime against which all else is measured – the un-comparable, to which all else is compared. With its recording in history, its recurrence also became possible.[23] Among other slogans, the demonstrators of 1968 shouted 'We are all German Jews', which for them meant the ultimate victims. The term 'Jew' seemed to have shifted from designating those who suffered a specific historical experience to indicating a universal position of victimhood.

The discourse of the Holocaust thereby functions similarly to the way that the idea of the 'state of nature' functions in the political philosophy of Hobbes and other modern political philosophers: an evil, the escape from which the entire political field must be dedicated. Nothing validates human rights and humanitarian action more than the cry 'never again.'[24]

Challenging Third Worldism

The connection between humanitarianism and the anti-totalitarian perspective led MSF to embrace two struggles: the first for humanitarianism and the second against 'third worldism' – a particularly French way of designating (or denigrating) an anti-Western thought-practice that sees the decolonizing 'third world' as the site for the realization of Marxist struggle.

The year 1984, when its teams were setting up in Ethiopia, marked a key moment in MSF's transformation. Some of the organization's leaders, notably Claude Malhuret, François Jean and Rony Brauman, established an institute called Liberté Sans Frontières (LSF), which was tasked with formulating the ideas that would frame the organization's actions in a larger context of political and cultural change. In its inaugural conference of January 1985, Challenging Third Worldism, Bruckner delivered the

Michael Buerk in the BBC broadcast from Korem, 23 October 1984.
Stills from Dangerous Pity, *Brauman and Margolin.*

keynote speech, entitled 'Third World, Guilt, Self-Hate'. Brauman delivered an introductory address in which he stated, 'Third Worldism promotes simple notions: The West has looted Third World resources and multinational corporations engage in evil actions . . . we must work to ensure that we do not offer blind or irrational support to despotic and authoritarian regimes . . . and aid democratic forces in the Third World.'[25] The spirit of the conference was polemic, and it led MSF-Belgium to cut all connections with MSF-France after a long legal process in which the former protested the creeping politicization of the latter's humanitarianism, which MSF-France eventually lost, along with its attempt to forbid MSF-Belgium to use the name MSF.[26] Years later Edward Said sharply ridiculed the logic of similar positions maintained by LSF at the time:

> Legions of writers who had supported Algerian and Vietnamese resistance denounced their early befuddlement and romanticism. The coloured people hadn't benefited enough from European enlightenment, they said; resistance to empire had bred a barbarous and xenophobic anti-Westernism; anti-democratic fanaticism and intolerance (of which 'Islamo-fascism' is an example) were homegrown products that had nothing to do with the white man.[27]

TV donations to Ethiopia, 1985.
Stills from Dangerous Pity, *Brauman and Margolin.*

It was true that anti-totalitarians, in their anti–third worldist incarnation, tended to forget that a substantial part of Hannah Arendt's very own *Origins of Totalitarianism* argued that imperialism was the crucial ingredient in twentieth-century totalitarianism.[28] Brauman, in retrospect, explains his former position with regret: 'we were fierce anti-Communists, maybe something like neo-cons those days; [we felt that] there was a real war to be waged against communism . . . and we were on the front line fighting with medical aid.'[29] MSF was certainly riding the wave of conservatism of the Reagan and Thatcher era – undoubtedly the other trend to which humanitarianism owes its current prominence. Indeed, the 1980s culture of privatization kick-started a process that gave birth to a multiplicity of 'sovereignty-free actors' worldwide. These were independent organizations and new social movements as varied as the feminist, peace and green movements in the 1970s, religious groups, humanitarian organizations, new businesses and guerrilla groups, all of whom positioned themselves on the international stage conducting 'private-sphere diplomacy', which refused the homogenization of a vague political struggle and engaged in actions that were previously the preserve of states only.[30]

This, then, was the state of political things and the state of mind of some European aid workers as they landed on the outskirts of Korem, on a windswept mountainous plateau in northern Ethiopia, on the margins of a brutal, ethnically inspired civil war.

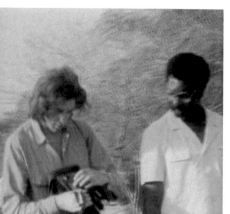

Bob Geldof with an Ethiopian government spokesperson. Stills from Dangerous Pity, *Brauman and Margolin.*

Humanitarian Optics

In September 1984, following the tenth anniversary celebrations of the Derg regime set up by Mengistu, an occasion that coincided with the famine, government censorship was eased and international journalists started gaining access to Ethiopia's rural areas. At the end of October the BBC was first to report from the famine's front line. Michael Buerk spoke from Korem of 'a biblical famine in the twentieth century.'[31] The war, he decided, was a side-story to the main issue: the unfolding humanitarian crisis of mass starvation. The theological imagery of a natural catastrophe emphasised the idea of famine as a simple, huge and apocalyptic concept. Buerk's broadcast undoubtedly helped provoke an unprecedented international reaction, but it also suited the aims of President Mengistu, who solicited international aid to buttress his control of the northern provinces. Incidentally, the report was also seen by Bob Geldof, who in response launched Band Aid at Christmas in 1984. After its success became apparent, Geldof also organized the televised rock concert Live Aid in July 1985. Proceeds went to organizations in Ethiopia, mainly to Christian Aid and Oxfam. Food aid flowed into the country at a rate of 100,000 tonnes a month, and humanitarians became media celebrities.[32]

When he travelled to Ethiopia, Geldof was received like a head of state by government officials. He started acting as their spokesperson, especially in defending their policies 'against the criticism of MSF', which irritated Geldof by its insistence on holding the Ethiopian government responsible for the famine and the allegation of deaths by forced deportation facilitated by international aid.[33] 'Your French philosophers have grown older and more conservative,' Geldof told *Le Monde*. 'They have lost the spark of humanity that the young have and they are betraying their youth . . . I will say it again: we want to be in every place people need us, without making distinctions. It is a duty, and morality is always above politics.'[34]

This 'criticism' of MSF was part of the organization's emphasis on 'speaking out' and 'bearing witness'. Testimony on behalf of victims was at the heart of a politically engaged humanitarianism that sought to extend its role, beyond the simple provision of medical relief, to publicly denouncing the forces which turned people into victims.[35] The story of 'humanitarian testimony' is of course now as commonplace as its critique. The founding aims of MSF, indeed, were articulated against the humanitarian model of the International Committee of the Red Cross. In contrast to the approach of organizations like MSF, the ICRC's pact with militaries and regimes was based on trading access to victims across military lines for the organization's discretion. It was an approach that led members of the ICRC to keep quiet about the gas chambers in Auschwitz, which they knew about as early as 1942.[36] More recently, but in the same vein, writers accused the ICRC of knowing – and keeping quiet about – the abuse of prisoners in Guantánamo Bay and Abu Ghraib, several months before these abuses became public knowledge. Defenders of the ICRC claim that the only reason that it could get to know about these violations in the first place was that it was granted access based on guarantees of secrecy – access which would undoubtedly be withdrawn if these guarantees were betrayed.

The ICRC also had a tradition of witnessing, one deriving from its Christian roots, which meant being in solidarity with those that suffer. Much of the work the ICRC provided on the battlefields of the late nineteenth and early twentieth centuries involved care of the dying, which was slow and painful, and aimed at arranging for a 'good death'. Nurses helped the dying pray, confess and write last letters.

In the early 1970s, in the shadow of slaughters in Pakistan/Bangladesh and Biafra, this tradition of testimony was politicized. In 1971 a physician with the ICRC in Biafra named Bernard Kouchner resigned after refusing to keep quiet about what he came to believe – wrongly, it turned out – was the Nigerian government's campaign to exterminate the Ibo population. It was in the face of the ICRC's strict codes of neutrality and discretion that Kouchner, later France's Foreign Minister, helped set up MSF. 'Speaking on behalf of victims and insisting on political responsibility' was framed as an anti-totalitarian act. Public testimony, whether written, filmed or audio-recorded, has become, alongside the delivery of aid, an integral part of the kind of humanitarianism that MSF promoted.[37] This adoption of testimony by humanitarian organizations, alongside many human rights ones, started the blurring of the borders between activism and journalism that is now commonplace.

Humanitarian action takes place amid war, and members of humanitarian groups experience violence firsthand. However, as Michal Givoni explained in her original study of humanitarian testimony, such testimony is only seldom based on direct eyewitness reports of events. More often than not, humanitarians speak from within aid compounds, and testify on the basis of the medical and mortality data they have gathered, and on the basis of what they have heard from their patients – often, in fact, on their behalf. In humanitarian missions, as the anthropologist Didier Fassin explains, 'the prolixity of humanitarianism increases in parallel to the silence of the survivor.'[38] Like the base at the town of Korem, humanitarian aid compounds became epistemic spaces – places in which most information about conflicts is gathered, and from which it is disseminated to the world. In the eyes of the general public, physicians have the credibility to speak not only about the medical condition of others, but also about the pain they suffer. Fassin takes to its logical conclusion the idea that testimony registers the subjective experience of violence. Because testimony is needed to foreground subjective experiences and because psychologists and psychiatrists 'have access to this subjectivity, they become the legitimate witnesses who speak in the name of those who have experienced the traumatic events'. Connecting the clinical and the subjective, Fassin has worked to make trauma one of the main registers for public testimony.[39] It is a form of testimony very different from ones delivered in a legal context. Tribunals and courts often demand a certain flattening of the testimony, the reduction of its traumatic register and emotive affect as well as all other issues that are in excess of a simple recreation of events.[40] Humanitarian testimonies, on the other hand, geared to popular media, tend to be more emotional than analytical. In its mediatization of suffering, humanitarian testimony – often presented alongside photographs of helpless children – also functions to compete for money in the charitable market, funds humanitarian agencies see as essential in providing the possibility for them to operate independently of government subsidy. In many respects it was the early phases of the tele-communications revolution and the increasing wealth of the globalizing markets of the 1980s that strengthened the cycle of empathy for faraway victims. The relation between humanitarians and media is thus one of interdependency: journalists – dependent on aid workers for access, trans-port, accommodation, information, telecommunications, sound bites and medical care – tend to narrate the events of a crisis from their point of view. Michael Buerk's visit to Ethiopia in July 1985 was accomplished through Oxfam; his report was based on data and information from British relief workers and MSF physicians.

The Testimony of the Dead

Emotional images and other forms of testimony might be essential when seeking to appeal for donations, but 'to have larger political effect in the international arena', Brauman explained, 'we needed to give clinical grounds to our appeal.'[41] This meant medical data would play a central role in the public statements of medical aid organizations. The presenta-tion of data extracted from the bodies of the injured or the deceased – such as toxic readings in blood samples, X-rays of broken bones, bullets taken out of patients' bodies, or the presentation of statistics of public health, nutrition and mortality of larger populations – became thus one of the most important tools of political advocacy. The most important element of these aspects of medical data was epidemiology – the statistical measuring and spatial mapping of patterns of public health and disease at the level of populations. Commonly, epidemiology is part of a scientific, evidence-based medical approach for identifying risk factors for disease, determining optimal approaches to treatment and evaluating medical needs and priorities.

For Brauman, epidemiology 'is the main dial in our dashboard, according to which we steer a mission.' But epidemiology has also become an important tool of advocacy. Data which might be incomprehensible from a single case study might present, at a collective level, statistical patterns that could be mobilised politically.

One of the public statements delivered by Brauman in an interview for *Paris Match* on 14 November 1985 – 'Fifty to a hundred thousand deaths in Ethiopia! Not through starvation, but through deportation!'[42] – was not based on eyewitness testimony or on interviews with patients, but on comparative mortality studies, undertaken by other organizations, that sought to demonstrate the extent of deaths from deportation. MSF's actions that led to its expulsion from Ethiopia were based on these secondhand calculations. In the wake of the Ethiopia mission, so that the organization could rely on its own data, Brauman set up an epidemiology unit within MSF, with its first case study being Afghanistan in the late 1980s.

The use of epidemiology supplemented testimony based on memory, trauma and speech with humanitarian testimony based in medical evidence in which statistics and the medical file became central. Because one of the main indicators for epidemiology is the mortality rate, its forms of enunciation shifted the subject of testimony from the living to the dead. Besides being 'medical experts' and ethical 'eyewitnesses', the nongovernmental humanitarians have, as Givoni put it, combined these two frames, and become 'expert witnesses' that speak from a specialized perspective of professional expertise and medical knowledge.

This type of 'speaking out' is articulated mainly through public reports. These reports often go against the mainstream political perceptions. Following the 1992 discovery of the camps in Bosnia, and before this became received knowledge, members of MSF conducted an inquiry with Bosnian refugees and used autopsy and medical evidence in a report that alleged 'crimes against humanity' – murder, torture and deportation – committed by Serb forces. This report was quoted in NATO's justification to sanction air strikes in Kosovo seven years later. If testimony, in its different forms, was one of the means to politicize humanitarianism, it seems to have also played a role in its militarization. More recently, however, MSF also acted in the opposite direction – to refute inflated claims of genocide. Within the heated debate on Darfur, where there was a strong political imperative to establish the actual figures of mortality, MSF came up with its own figures, and – contrary to the assertions of the human rights campaign Save Darfur and a host of public figures – it protested claims that the massacres in Darfur amounted to genocide, with the calls for Western intervention that were bound up in such a designation.[43]

This broadening of the notion of 'humanitarian testimony' from unmediated eyewitness account to include the presentation of medical evidence by expert witnesses could have logically led MSF to give its work a forensic dimension in national and international courts. However, this did not take place. In 1992, a year after the fall of Mengistu, a major trial for the 'crimes against humanity' of the previous regime was organized in Addis Ababa. Rony Brauman, still president of MSF, and Brigitte Vasset, still director of operations, received invitations to testify for the prosecution but declined because they considered the process to be 'a political trial' that would abuse their testimony for purposes that had nothing to do with humanitarianism. Anyway, in their opinion, the crisis had by then already ended, and there was no role for humanitarians to play in relation to this process.

Although MSF actively supported the creation of the International Criminal Court, it later decided not to testify before it. One aspect of the problem MSF perceived in this court was the growing institutionalization of international humanitarian law. The legalization of armed conflict – starting with the creation of the International Criminal Tribunal for the former Yugoslavia (ICTY) in 1993, followed by the International Criminal Tribunal for Rwanda (ICTR) in 1994, and culminating in the establishment of the permanent International Criminal Court (ICC) in 1998, all with mandates to prosecute war crimes, crimes against humanity and genocide – posed fundamental challenges to the practice of humanitarian testimony and evidence. The 'agora centrism' of international tribunals meant that they became saturated with media attention in the way that courts – still largely allergic to media presence – were not allowed to be. 'The ICC imposed new constraints on the way we express ourselves in the public sphere,' Brauman notes. 'Since the ICC was established we have become aware that anything we say on our Web site or in press releases could find its way to the prosecutors. In particular, medical files and mortality data became a valuable element for indictment . . . so this became a problem.' Brauman also repeats the predicament that the ICRC found – and continues to find – itself in: 'When parties on the ground think of MSF staff as potential witnesses, they will limit our access, safety and independence.'[44]

Testimony, for Brauman, should not be thought of in relation to human rights or international law, accountability or justice, that often come *post factum*, but rather in relation to attempts to change events as they are taking place, and also as part of a humanitarian necessity to help stir the mission in relation to availability of limited means.

MSF's alternative to the delivery of testimony in the forums of international justice is to provide its patients with individual medical certificates that might be used as evidence in court, should the patients decide to press charges after independently evaluating the risks and benefits of doing so.

Although to a large extent MSF is identified with the delivering of independent public testimony, Brauman explained that 'the prominence of this form of address started declining after the Ethiopia mission'. Not only did it lead to expulsion of MSF from the country but, given the aid agency's active participation in the perpetuating of the crisis, it lacked the self-critique necessary to realize the level of responsibility of the humanitarians themselves to the calamities. The controversy over its involvement in Ethiopia initiated a shift from MSF's obligation as a bystanding witness to the crimes of others to the consideration of its own responsibility as an actor. Brauman explains: 'Being critical of forced relocation and being compassionate towards the people who are forcibly relocated is not enough, because nobody cares. Instead of focusing on the crimes committed by a Stalinist regime, we entered a new stage in our critical thinking: we began to reflect more seriously upon our role, upon the potential negative consequences of our activity – upon the fact that we could inadvertently play into the hands of agencies whose objectives had nothing to do with humanitarianism.'[45]

The focus of interrogation has turned inwards, and critique has turned into self-critique, somewhat inspired by the tradition of auto-critique maintained by the former 'Maos'. It was based on the realization that aid participates in, perpetuates, transforms and manipulates crisis: that the very presence of humanitarian missions changes the dynamic of the conflict into which they are inserted.

The MSF think tank, LSF, which was dedicated to ideological and political thinking, closed in 1987. It was succeeded by an organization promoting expert research – the Centre de Réflexion sur l'Action et les Savoirs Humanitaires (CRASH) – which was established to stimulate action-oriented research for examining the role of humanitarians in crisis areas.

Armies of Compassion

Bernard Kouchner, who was originally as in favour of Biafran secession as de Gaulle's government had been in the early 1970s, has grown to believe that political and military force should be placed at the service of humanitarian ideals.[46] In 1988, following his appointment as French President Mitterrand's secretary of state for humanitarian affairs, his early achievement was to have codified the *droit d'ingérence* – the right to disregard national sovereignty, and to intervene in countries experiencing 'natural disasters and similar emergency situations', which he had begun to develop a few years earlier with the law professor Mario Bettati.[47] The category of 'similar to natural disaster' was a politically useful way to include in the resolution the right to interfere in situations of war. Indeed, this very principle was invoked by the UN Security Council when opening a 'humanitarian corridor' for Kurds fleeing Iraq in 1990 and 1991. It was also the seed that would later grow into the *responsibility to protect* (R2P) – the right/duty to intervene in order to prevent and stop crimes against humanity and genocide, codified in a 2005 UN resolution with the support of the George W. Bush administration.[48]

With genocide being the trigger for all forms of intervention, Kouchner started to identify many instances of 'crimes against humanity' – not only retrospectively in Biafra, but also in Kosovo and Darfur. 'Influenced by his friend Bernard-Henri Lévy, Kouchner's worldview was schematized in the extreme,' one of his more critical biographers writes. 'It is an easy world to figure out. All you need to do is separate heroes and villains, good and evil, civilization and barbarism, and, finally, victims and perpetrators.'[49] Most recently, Darfur became the site of a contemporary holocaust where evil confronted good. In 2004, none other than the US Holocaust Memorial Museum blew the whistle of genocide, leading to the unanimous resolution of both houses of the US Congress to 'seriously consider multilateral or even unilateral intervention to prevent genocide' if the UN Security Council failed to act.[50] In 2005 a movement calling for an end to mass killing in Darfur included the US Congressional Black Caucus, evangelicals, neoconservatives, and human rights and student activist groups. The humanitarian position seemed to have continuously fluctuated between paranoia and megalomania.

Bob Geldof also reappeared with 'an initiative to put Darfur on the same continuum as Auschwitz and Srebrenica',[51] while Bernard-Henri Lévy, referring to Darfur as 'the first genocide of the twenty-first century', called for enforcement of the arrest warrant imposed on President Omar al-Bashir of Sudan for 'crimes against humanity', even if it required, as it would have, outright military intervention.[52] This conjunction of minds was sealed with the announcement in 2010 that Bob Geldof will play the role of BHL in a film, *Mauvaise Fille*, directed by the latter's daughter.

In the post–Cold War conflicts that erupted in the Balkans and in central Africa, aid agencies moved closer towards an openly partisan form of humanitarianism. Given international inaction over the massacres in Rwanda and Bosnia, and the way in which European leaders described the massacres as 'humanitarian disasters' – a designation that allowed them to use humanitarian missions as a pretext for avoiding political and military responses – a number of leading agencies, Oxfam and some parts of MSF included, started to lobby for military intervention. It was a call that blurred the difference between those humanitarian organizations that saw their role as the relief of suffering and human rights groups that concentrated on calls for accountability; accordingly, these two kinds of organization started to draw increasingly closer, gradually blurring into the 'integrated' humanitarian–political–legal approach now favoured by the UN and many nongovernmental organizations.

*   *   *

A few years after NATO's defeat of Serbia in Kosovo, humanitarianism and politics coincided under Kouchner's leadership as the head of the United Nations Interim Administration Mission in Kosovo, where their roles also completely overlapped. Under Kouchner's leadership, humanitarians, human rights groups and militaries shared both aims and compounds in their rebuilding of Kosovo as an autonomous province, and the infrastructure of the state to come.

From the political perspective, the history of humanitarian intervention appears like a series of inversions and overcompensations: the failure in 1993 of the US humanitarian–military intervention in Somalia made the Clinton administration recoil from military action to halt the Rwanda genocide in 1994. Criticism of the US failure to act prompted Clinton to commit troops to halt the Serbian attack in Kosovo five years later. The lessons Tony Blair drew from that conflict encouraged him to support the invasion of Iraq in 2003 on humanitarian grounds. The failure to get international mandate for the Iraq invasion led the Franco-British initiative in Libya to seek international mandate in the spring of 2011. In the wake of these bombings, Nicolas Sarkozy claimed that this drive for humanitarian intervention based on R2P was a 'new model for world governance', but this model has already been in the making for years.

In recent decades the independent humanitarian sector has also expanded. While in 1980 there were about 40 NGOs dealing with the Ethiopian famine, a decade later 250 were operating during the Yugoslavian war; by 2004, 2,500 were involved in Afghanistan.[53] The larger and more influential the humanitarian world has grown, the more incoherent it has become. As the humanitarian movement became more openly partisan and political, governments around the world began recasting their own political projects and military adventures as humanitarian ones. The term 'humanitarianism' came to be used in relation to any provision of medical, shelter and food aid – even if these were undertaken by militaries or by state agencies following political agendas. The search for proximity was mutual. Military intervention was justified in humanitarian terms. Humanitarian commands, a branch of the military dealing with issues of aid of all sorts, have been set up in most Western militaries with some advice from international NGOs. Finally, humanitarian organizations have become increasingly dependent on militaries in order to gain access to civilians in unsecured areas.

Food transport to Ethopia. Stills from Dangerous Pity, *Brauman and Margolin.*

Soldiers in what George W. Bush has called 'the armies of compassion' themselves became proxy experts in this kind of humanitarianism, while military airdrops of food and medicine in war zones became an integral part of the war effort. This conjunction was articulated in a statement made by Colin Powell in 2001 to the effect that NGOs and relief workers are 'a force multiplier for us . . . an important part of our combat team,'[54] and later echoed by Tony Blair who called for robust 'military–humanitarian coalitions'. After the fall of Baghdad in 2003, American NGOs funded via USAID were informed by the US administration that 'their cooperation was inextricably linked to America's strategic goals.'[55] The same was also true of British funding for overseas aid and humanitarian groups after the coalition government took power in 2010. This blurring of roles meant that in places such as Afghanistan, Chechnya, Sri Lanka and Sudan, belligerents started to construe aid workers as enemies, an integral part of the occupying force, a view that inevitably led to an increase in the kidnapping and murder of humanitarians.

In East Africa, the aid infrastructure of the late Cold War expanded into the aid infrastructure of the war on terror, which now extended over Yemen, Somalia, Sudan, Chad, Mauritania and Mali, as is demonstrated by the centrality of development aid for some of these countries in the 2005 Pentagon-run Africa Command's Trans-Sahara Counter-Terrorism Initiative. Meles Zenawi, the rebel TPLF leader who overthrew Mengistu

in 1991, is still the Prime Minister of Ethiopia, a nominally Christian country surrounded by largely Islamic Somalia, Sudan and Kenya, which has also become a key ally in the 'war on terror'. Since Meles took power, his government has received about $26 billion in development aid, more than any other nation in sub-Saharan Africa.

Minima Moralia

'During the Bosnia war I was at a crossroads. On the one hand I continued to pursue positions inherited from the Cold War; on the other, I was trying to get my bearings in the new world we were suddenly living in after the Berlin wall came down,' Brauman told the philosopher and publisher Michel Feher in a famous interview. Brauman went on to note that at the beginning of the wars of former Yugoslavia, 'we were very explicitly influenced by Hannah Arendt, [as] Bosnia seemed like the traditional confrontation between liberal democracy and totalitarianism . . . and I responded in the liberal way, by raising the flag of human rights.'[56] But as raising the flag of human rights meant military intervention, this position also clashed with Brauman's aversion to a humanitarianism that could be absorbed into state politics and military strategy.[57] Moreover, he thought making public MSF's opinion on juridical categories such as ' "crimes against humanity" – which has always had an implicit reference to the Nazi camps – has political, military and legal consequences beyond our control. The language one uses both frames the problem and determines the kind of response. To say "crimes against humanity" is to call for immediate military intervention to stop it – and this is beyond the mandate of humanitarianism.'[58]

It the face of this bold humanitarian vision, with its violent cosmopolitan order of geopolitical statements and calls for humanitarian intervention, Brauman started to promote humanitarianism in its minimalist form, humanitarianism as the practice of 'lesser evils'. The 'lesser evil', in the way that Brauman refers to it, is a humanitarianism that sustains life without seeking to govern or manage populations, without making political claims on their behalf, or seeking to resolve root causes of conflicts. It is a humanitarianism that unashamedly and impartially deals with the problems of 'bare life'. This concept, designating the vulnerability of a life stripped out of any civil and political rights that might protect it, comes out of the work of the philosopher Giorgio Agamben and has in recent years been popularized in the context of the critique of humanitarian action.[59] In what might be defined as the critique of the critique of humanitarianism, Brauman made sure to adopt the very terms by which he was criticized: 'of course, we take care of the bodies. We as aid workers try to maintain life . . . I would, on the contrary, feel very uncomfortable if we were trying to do more – to control or penetrate people's minds. What people ask us, what they expect from us, is to help them survive. For the rest, they can manage by themselves.'[60] 'Upholding a vision of humanitarianism as the policy of the lesser evil', in Brauman's view, in the meaning of the quote that began this chapter, is a temporary autonomous act of solicitude that 'is about little more than the caring for bodies.' Politics based in medicine, he states, must be abandoned in exchange for the obvious: the actual practice of humanitarianism and clinical medicine. It is in this sense that 'accepting the policy of the lesser evil . . . becomes one of the ways to live with the contradiction [of humanitarianism] without completely becoming a victim of it.'[61]

But this is a different conception of the 'lesser evil' argument than the one Brauman rejected in his withdrawal from Ethiopia, where it concerned collaboration with 'totalitarians'. It is also different to that articulated by the likes of Kouchner and Lévy, who conceive the idea from the point of view of the state and Western values, in the context of fighting in the name of the 'lesser evil' of democracy, and finally it is also different from the 'ethical realism' of Michael Ignatieff, in which the practice of 'the lesser evil' demands the imposition of ethical constraints on states' actions while in the pursuit and defence of 'moral goals' such as freedom, human rights and democracy.[62]

Against what Brauman calls the 'imperial policy of humanitarianism', his meaning of 'the lesser evil' designates the project of humanitarianism at its most minimal – as one that 'takes no political stand, makes no claim to transform society, and doesn't come to make war or peace, promote economic development, help administer justice, or export democracy or human rights values.'[63] These, he thinks, are not necessarily bad things in themselves, but they are the responsibility of the politicians and have little to do with humanitarianism as such, which in its minimal, independent, impartial and barest meaning should seek to provide nothing more than immediate, short-term relief and medical aid, which David Rieff, following Bertolt Brecht, called 'a bed for the night'. Such humanitarianism 'won't change the world' – nor does it seek to.[64]

The search for independence from existing political forces and the rejection of the use of the Holocaust to understand contemporary politics – much like the rejection of the ethical designation of 'victims' and 'perpetrators' – also imply that physicians working in conflict zones recover the term 'patient' and with it the basic terms of the Hippocratic oath, in which the only category that a physician should be concerned with is the clinical. Humanitarianism is not, of course, limited to a medical practice, it also concerns the conditions needed for medical practice to function independently and impartially; but political deliberations and priorities should remain radically external to this situation, which is clinical. Observers have commented that this seems like a return to a rather classic Red Cross stance.[65] In effect this stance is a radicalization of the ICRC mandate. The ICRC describes its humanitarian mission as comprising four basic elements: protection, prevention, assistance and cooperation. The first two categories involve dialogue with parties in conflict about the manner in which they conduct themselves.[66] The lesser-evil-humanitarianism argument makes no such claims. It is necessary for medical professionals to operate across the world, like it is necessary to have hospitals in towns and cities – but this does not mean that emergency medicine must be the ground for a cosmopolitan liberal political project.

Aid Archipelago

This minimal approach to humanitarianism has found its spatial manifestation in what Brauman called a 'humanitarian space'. In his conception the humanitarian space is a form of spatial practice rather than an actual space or a territorial designation. Against the tendency of conflicts since the 1980s to generate integrated and entangled political–military–humanitarian spaces, mainly around refugee camps, this space is conceived in order to hold relief work at a distance from political and military practice.

Brauman's conception of the humanitarian space is different from the way it is currently designated and practised by UN agencies such as UNHCR (United Nations High Commission for Refugees) or OCHA (Office for the Coordination of Humanitarian Affairs). In the latter case, humanitarian spaces are clusters of extraterritorial enclaves and the protected corridors that connect them with infrastructure and transport centres. These kinds of humanitarian spaces are often marked as circles on maps around the areas where relief operations take place – at 'the internal peripheries of war'. Within them the UN establishes 'integrated platforms' that combine different organizations pursuing each a different task in the division of labour of contemporary emergencies: international law, economic development, migration control, and 'peacekeeping' if necessary. This is akin to a government by experts with different aspects of refugee life catered for by a wide multiplicity of highly specialised international organizations and aid agencies. This form of 'relief-sovereignty', as Brauman cynically refers to it, can be imposed by the UN on weak states and on those not in effective control of their territories. Although professing neutrality and impartiality, the management of these spaces tends to be aligned with the political objectives of the UN or of the members of the Security Council.[67]

Driving the humanitarian present is no longer a sense of naive but dangerous compassion, but rather a highly specialized and concerted international effort to manage populations that are seen as posing risk. In his work on the refugee camps of Africa, the anthropologist Michel Agier, refers to contemporary humanitarianism as nothing less than 'a distant and delegated form of management, a government without citizens'.[68] He describes the humanitarian zones as heavily guarded and tightly policed 'waiting rooms on the margins of the world', built and maintained for the purpose of the 'total government of the planet's populations who are most unwanted and undesirable'. In them the well-meaning humanitarians 'find themselves acting as low-cost managers of exclusion on a planetary scale.'[69] Refugee camps are part of an overall system of migration control, he says, intended to provide for displaced populations at a distance from western shores. They are islands in an archipelago of extraterritoriality, which also includes extended border control practices and detention centres. The earlier obsession of humanitarianism with identifying and sorting out perpetrators from victims is here rendered irrelevant as both categories morph into that of the potential migrant, whose entry into western countries cannot be countenanced and must be stopped at any price. Displaced populations become the concern of the international community precisely because of the risks they potentially pose. The fear of migration, crime and terrorism is concieved of as being in inverse relation to the well-being of populations. This tendency is best captured by the term 'human security' under which every dimension of human life – from food and shelter to education – is measured within a shifting calculus of risk.

In Brauman's conception, humanitarian spaces are not territorial zones, but rather sets of operational categories, or space-bound circumstantial conditions, that make independent humanitarian work possible. In the absence of such conditions a mission might become counterproductive and relief organizations would do better not to operate, or be forced to withdraw, when these no longer exist.

Foremost among the criteria for such a zone is that it should remain at a distance from armies, militias and political officials, a principle that should equally apply to the 'liberal armies of compassion' and to 'third world totalitarians'.[70]

However, humanitarian spaces must allow the approximate attainment of a number of other basic 'freedoms'. As Brauman has put it: 'the humanitarian space is primarily a way of measuring the humanitarian conditions. They are not absolutes. How freely you can talk to patients, how freely you can move around or go to other places to see the problems, how freely you can monitor the delivery and distribution of goods. I am not deluding myself. I know this will never be perfect, that we are always within power relations. So the humanitarian space is a tool for measuring our distance from powers.'[71]

Deliberately steering away from involvement with states, international organizations whose aims are other than humanitarian (international development or international law), militaries and militias is a laborious process that requires constant manoeuvring between political forces. Evading the political requires an understanding of the logic of politics as much as evading the military requires understanding the logic of military action.[72] This makes it necessary for humanitarians to engage in constant analytical reflection upon the situation as it develops. Brauman explains: 'This is not about being political, or looking for political effect, but about understanding the political force-field on the ground and our place within it. We produce our analysis, which combines medical and political data, in order to help us guide the mission, to minimize political effects, and not in order to intervene in politics.'[73] The production and mobilization of information by these humanitarians is no longer an ethical act of communicating compassion, mobilizing shame or speaking truth to power, but rather a set of analytic reflections that aim to help decipher the political impact of the humanitarian organization's own actions within the general dynamics of the crisis, and to provide an operational guidelines to help designate and protect the humanitarian space.[74]

Polis and the Police

A humanitarian space may sometimes grow and solidify, giving rise to camps: these then form a material link between humanitarianism and a massive and rapid process of migration, construction and quasi-urbanization.

There is, at present, according to UN figures, a worldwide whirlwind of displacement affecting about 75 million people. Of these, 12 million are refugees recognized by the UNHCR, with at least 4 million living in refugee camps. Of the rest, some 30 million people are what the UN refers to as Internally Displaced Persons – displaced by war or violence, but, like many in Afghanistan, Iraq or Sudan, still within the border of their state of citizenship. At least 6 million people from this category live in camps. Together with the Palestinian refugee camps, some 12 million people are currently living in about one thousand camps worldwide.[75] Regardless of their geographical dispersal and number, the physical design of refugee camps, according to original research by the architect Manuel Herz, originates from a single UN design manual applied and adapted in different contexts. After crossing an international border, the fleeing inhabitants of entire territories are processed by humanitarians and organized into a dense and sometimes segregated fabric of districts, blocks and shelters. These camps are planned according to medical principles, a combination of makeshift hospitals for the mass treatment of large populations, and military camps for disciplined control. Hygiene, sanitation, the management and containment of plague, the circulation of services, infrastructure and the provision of water, electricity, medicine and nutrition, along with the disposal of sewage and waste, all become the organizational principles of a new spatial regime of multiple separations and regimentation of time and space, intersecting quasi-military with quasi-medical principles.[76] Financed by international organizations such as the European Commission's Humanitarian Aid Department, the UN itself, or national organizations such as USAID and, of course, millions of private donors, these spaces are woven into the global network of commodity circulation through the products of aid and to the international networks of information flow through the media.

Herz demonstrates the rapidity with which humanitarian zones can solidify into a quasi-urban environment. Within days of relocation of the refugees from their homes, barter and commerce is established. Within weeks, markets evolve to exchange goods and labour between the refugees and the citizens of the host country. Within several months, clusters and districts turn into a 'neighbourhood', and rows of prefabricated shelters made of provisional materials such as plastic sheeting become solid structures of wooden huts, adobe, brick or corrugated metals laid out in a dense fabric of districts and blocks that condenses in miniature complex geographies of origin by their internal regions and divisions. The loss of homes, villages and towns, the construction of and accommodation to newly built environments, the first encounter with a multiplicity of different cultures, languages and technologies, aid workers and journalists, lead to a situation that upsets old social and family hierarchies and inspires new political desires. Emergency, in the words of the humanitarian scholar Alex de Waal, 'fuels the locomotive of history, accelerating socio-economic change.'[77] Dadaab, in 1999 still a semi-arid Kenyan market town of a few thousand, has now – after UNHCR established a series of refugee camp around it – one of the world's largest concentrations of displaced people, more than 450,000, including also a great multiplicity of international aid and development workers.

Extraterritorial humanitarian spaces are perforated by other extraterritorial bubbles within them. 'Trucks, four-wheel drive vehicles, walkie-talkies, satellite phones, and computers create an artificial environment, whose perverse effect is to put the teams in a quasi-virtual world where time and space are measured in different units from those of the country where they find themselves. So they find themselves, almost without knowing it, in a bubble, a "non-place", a humanitarian mission which could be everywhere and which is nowhere.'[78]

There are also peripheral bubbles, enclaves of those excluded from the excluded, lying at the margins of camps – these are the haphazard accommodations of the internally displaced persons who cannot be given treatment by international organizations because, although displaced by violence or need, they are still within their state of citizenship and have not crossed an international border to merit the status of refugee and with it international attention. They sometimes establish improvised encampments near the edges of refugee camps in order to feed off whatever left over services or secondarily traded aid materiel may come their way.

But while aid and aid workers move in and out of the zone, the displaced and the refugees are often imprisoned in it, or stay in the camps because they have nowhere else to go, or haven't the means to go there. Although in some of their features, such as density, scale, trade, services and social life, camps can approximate an urban environment, and sometimes might appear as a town, they do so without being proper political spaces: they are governed spaces, which lack the political capacity for self-government and cannot be considered a polis – a city.

Michel Agier convincingly argues that the depoliticized nature of humanitarian zones inevitably excludes refugees from politics. 'The camp does not need democracy in order to function,'[79] says a humanitarian manager, quoted by Agier, in the Tobanda camp, in Sierra Leone, in November 2003. This leads Agier to suggest that the connection between the emergency medical assistance of humanitarianism and the architectural impetus for camp making should be broken. Aid without a camp is aid that does not seek to manage, house, develop and perform migration control. Refugees, like all people escaping war and famine throughout history, make their way across borders into cities, or settle and construct new ones. Aid, if necessary, should follow them into these spaces rather than construct environments of total control to facilitate its delivery.[80]

Whether in camps or in shantytonws, the separation of the humanitarian sphere from the political should be conceived in a way that supports the politics of the dispaced themselves. In fact, the more politically limited the aims of the humanitarian mission, the better the chance for politics to emerge independently. Thomas Keenan has shown how to understand the potential asymmetry between these forms of depoliticization and politicization. These terms, he claims, are not necessarily opposites – indeed, each might refer to a different kind of politics. 'Sometimes politics must be suspended in order to find a different route back into it', he says. 'By evacuating the camp of one form of politics, another may open up, a more primal one: one that reclaims the right to politics, to practise it oneself, and not to be the political object of others.'[81]

This realization is already implied in the ideas that Brauman expressed in the interviews that led to this chapter, but its implications will have to be radicalized if the politics of humanitarianism are to give ground to the politics of the displaced. Humanitarianism should indeed aim to provide no more than the bare minimum to support the revival of life after violence and destruction. As long as refugees are alive, the potential for political transformation still exists. The very life of refugees, their life as refugees, poses a potent political claim with transformative potential, one that represents a fundamental challenge to the states and state system that keep them displaced. This is the reason that generations of political leaders, from the Democratic Republic of the Congo through to Kosovo and Palestine, emerge from among the refugees to become the vanguard of political struggles. The refugees' return to politics has unpredictable consequences, which are and must always remain beyond the horizons of humanitarians and aid groups. Only when humanitarianism seeks to offer temporary assistance rather than to govern or develop can the politics of humanitarianism really create a space for the politics of refugees themselves. This shift demands that we think about the politics of aid not only from the perspective of the paradoxes and dilemmas of the relief workers and the people that send them, not only concerning the problems of humanitarian cooption, evasion, government and refusal, but primarily from the question of the politics of refugees, their claims, their rights and their potential actions, their wishes, their exercise and their evasion of power, their potential return. It might be that only with the ultimate refusal of aid at a time of their choice – with the rejection of the very apparatus that sometimes keeps them in good health, and sometimes operates to manage their exclusion – with refugees constructing their own spaces, self governing, posing demands and acting upon them – that the potentiality of their political life will actualize. Then, where there were camps there could be cities.

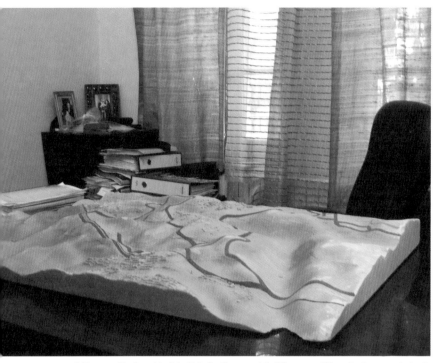

A Topographical model of the Beit Surik area with different possible walls drawn on it, in the office of Adv. Muhammad Dahla. Photo: Eyal Weizman, 2008.

3

The Best of All Possible Walls

In a diary entry written during his time as an Austrian soldier in World War I, Ludwig Wittgenstein noted the following incident. In a trench on the Russian front he found a magazine that described a court case in Paris involving an accident between a truck and a baby's pram. At the trial a scale model was presented. The relation between the truck, the pram and the people involved was represented by miniatures and dolls. Wittgenstein, who was, a few years later, to engage in architecture, became fascinated by this model. Because the representative elements in it – the street, houses, cars and people – bore a scale relation to things in reality, Wittgenstein thought that the model was a good example of the structure of language. Not only did it illustrate the language by which the trial was conducted, the model was a proposition; that is, a description of a possible state of affairs. The only thing missing, he thought, was the pain. It then occurred to Wittgenstein that one might reverse the analogy – that a proposition might itself serve as a model that could structure reality.[1]

Wittgenstein's reflection on the way a model was able to illustrate legal language might help shed some light on the story that follows, a story that is itself engaged with acts of translation, undertaken in court, from reality to its representation on a physical model, and vice versa.

The series of legal challenges against Israel's separation wall in the Israeli High Court involved cross-examinations conducted around a territorial scale model. These processes have already been exhaustively analyzed by legal experts. But in what follows, the story is told from the perspective of its object-participant – the model itself. Significantly, the legal processes involving the wall were trials not of people, but rather of an apparatus – it was the wall itself that was on trial. The model was thus not presented as evidence to help establish the guilt or innocence of the actions of the wall's planners and builders – rather, it helped arrive at a verdict on the 'behaviour' of the wall itself. Proportionality was the principle employed to evaluate this behaviour. In this process the different material aspects of the apparatus were regulated and fine-tuned within the legal forum and according to the terms of proportionality. The process helped establish what the state later regarded as a 'correct' proportion between conflicting principles – security requirements for Israelis as argued by military lawyers, and issues of 'livelihood' to Palestinians as argued by humanitarian representatives. In other words, the trials were concerned with moderating the violations and violence perpetrated by the wall in the name of the principle of the 'lesser evil'.

In the winter of 2004 Muhammad Dahla, a prominent Jerusalem-based Palestinian lawyer, was involved in two major court cases. One took place under the aegis of the International Court of Justice (ICJ) in The Hague, where as a legal adviser to the Palestinian team he helped appeal against the authority of the state to build a wall on the occupied West Bank; the other, at the Israeli High Court of Justice (HCJ) in Jerusalem, where, on behalf of several landowners from the Palestinian village of Beit Sourik, an agricultural village north-west of Jerusalem, he helped appeal against the segments of the route that were to leave them separated from about 300 acres of their fields.[2] In both cases, I should add, I had a minor involvement – a map I produced was presented as an evidence.

The second commission arrived as a result of the first. Seeing Dahla interviewed on Al Jazeera, Beit Sourik villagers rang him on his mobile phone while he was still in The Hague. Dahla did not immediately consent to represent them. The case posed an age-old dilemma: was working with the Israeli legal system to alleviate the excesses of the occupation worth the price in legitimizing it?

Dahla is one of the most influential of a generation of Palestinian legal activists to emerge from within areas of Palestine lost to Israel in 1948. He is one of the founders and former chair (1997–2000) of Adalah, the legal centre for Arab rights.[3] He has represented such prominent political

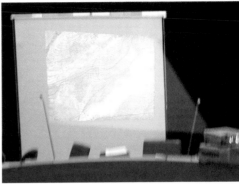

Militry lawyers and the team of Adv. Muhammad Dahla setting up presentations in the High Court of Justice in Jerusalem, a few minutes before proceedings begin. Photo: Bimkom, 2004.

figures as Azmi Bishara, the founder and leader of the National Democratic Alliance, a party of which he is a member. The Alliance was formed in 1995 in opposition to the Oslo Accords. Its platform is to struggle to transform the state of Israel into a democracy for all its citizens, and not only for its Jewish majority. Through Adalah and his private office, Dahla's decision to work with the institutions of the Israeli state is based on a rational-instrumental decision. He selected his cases on the grounds that they constitute precedent-setting legal challenges that expose paradoxes between the state's democratic pretence and its colonial realities.[4] It was an attempt to exercise a form of immanent critique in which the law itself becomes the object of political contestation. But this often backfired.

On his return to Jerusalem Dahla took the villagers' case. And so it happened that 'at the same time,' as he explained, 'I had to appeal against the illegality of the entire wall in The Hague and against the details of its execution in Jerusalem.'[5] Whereas in The Hague the issue had been argued in relatively abstract terms, and the advisory process established the illegality of the wall *tout court*, in the High Court of Justice in Jerusalem the case had to engage with the physical details of planning and implementation. Dealing with the project segment by segment, the case examined such details as prefabricated concrete elements, barbed wire and wire meshes, the layout of villages, the slopes of hills and road works, irrigation basins, fields and orchards, lines of sight and ranges of different weapons.

The robotic CNC computer milling of a topographical model. Photo: Eyal Weizman, 2008.

To argue their position both parties used different means of representation: topographic maps, plans, aerial and satellite imagery, photographs
and video documentation together with their associated means of display.
Frustrated by not being able to comprehend the crucial details of the case,
the judges suspended the trial for ten days, demanding – much as an
architecture professor might do of her students – that the petitioners
return with physical scale models.

Aided by a group of planning-rights activists, Dahla's team, unskilled
in the art of model-making and initially unsure about how to proceed, had
the model produced by a company that specialized in making terrain
models for the military. The model-maker explained the benefit of the
inversion: 'having worked for the military we understood the logic of how
they think . . . [The trial] was a war game, with the two sides, playing on
the same terrain, each seeking to beat the other.'[6] The model's production
would be the first in a series of inversions. It was made in a computer-
controlled milling process in high-density foam. It was then painted,
'emphasising the topography, fields and orchards'[7] that were the concern
of the petitioners, and delivered to Dahla's office. And so, the first model
of the wall to have ever been produced was not made by the party erecting
the wall, but rather by those opposing it.

On the weekend before the proceedings recommenced, Dahla met
with a group of retired Israeli security officials called the Peace and
Security Council (PSC). A few weeks earlier they received the status of
amici curiae – 'friends of the court' – a term which designated volunteers
offering expert information to assist the court in deciding matters before
it.[8] They tried to help Dahla understand some 'practical security necessities' of barrier design, in order that he could effectively argue for an
alternative to the wall as designed by the state. 'It was like a military
seminar', Dahla recalled. 'I was taking a crash course in military and security terminology, learning terms like "controlling elevation", which is a
high place that poses a threat, "ballistic weapons" as opposed to "flat
trajectory weapons" . . . it was very complicated but at the end I felt I
could become a general in the Palestinian army!'[9]

As they set about advising Dahla, the former officers drew different lines
on the model. In red, they drew the line along which Israeli security contractors had started to erect the wall. In blue, they drew another line, an
alternative wall whose route was less invasive than the red one but nevertheless still a wall – 'a lesser evil alternative' they called it, which left a larger
proportion of fields in Palestinian hands. Dahla, who didn't agree that the
line drawn by the officers sufficiently minimized the Israeli state's infringement on the Beit Sourik villagers' lands, or simply averse to accepting the
position of former generals, drew yet another blue line, one running even
closer to the Green Line: the border of 1967. In our conversation Dahla
stressed that his line should not be mistaken for 'an actual proposal for
another wall,' but rather as a tactical move: 'we drew the other line in order
to show the court that even according to the security concept presented by
the army there exists the possibility for a "less drastic mean" – another possible route that can cause less harm to the villagers . . . and that on the basis of
this the court should declare the red [state] route illegal.'

On one or two occasions the blue line that he drew crossed the Green
Line into Israeli territory. 'The army said that the Green Line is irrelevant,
that the route of the wall is dictated only by security and topographical
considerations, and I wanted to render this argument absurd, and in some
areas I drew the blue line on the Israeli side of the Green Line because the
topography there was better from a security perspective. If the international
border is irrelevant, it must be irrelevant both ways . . . and the state

A topographical model of the Beit Surik area with different possible walls. In red is the route built by the government, in blue is the "lesser evil" line. Note that the blue line crosses the green line. Photo: Eyal Weizman, 2008.

should confiscate land from Israelis [in order to build it] – in fact, why not?'[10]

When, ten days later, the court reconvened, Dahla brought the model into court. The Supreme Court Building in Jerusalem had been completed in the early 1990s. With its abundant allusions to the biblical, mystical and Jerusalem vernacular, it has won much national and some international acclaim with those who favour the excesses of postmodernism. It is a well-appointed building, but it has made no special provision for the presentation of architectural models, perhaps because the juridical role of the high court is usually not in the examination of evidence.

Dahla recalled that the porters who carried the model in 'went around in circles not knowing where to place it'. Somebody had an idea: a table was hurried in from the building's cafeteria and placed in front of the judges' bench. Dahla recalled that because the judges' bench was too high and the

Porters bringing the model into the High Court of Justice in Jerusalem, Beit Surik case 2004.
Illustration: Christine Cornell [with Eyal Weizman] 2008.

table too low, the judges could not see the model from where they sat, and
that they had to step down to look at it properly. The judges also called the
lawyers from both parties to join them. Petitioners, respondents and judges
assembled around the model. Some people approached from the audience to
better hear the discussion. The court descended into momentary disorder.
The physical presence of the model disturbed the legal protocol, and introduced its own rules of language. Later, Dahla recalled, 'All of a sudden, no one
was using terms such as "your honour" or "my learned friend".' Shulamit
Hartman, one of the activists who helped Dahla with the production of the
model and was present in court that day, observed: 'the presence of the model
introduced very dramatic changes to the courtroom. The usual structure and
"order" was disrupted and there was an unordered conversation.' People like

Parties to the process leave their places and assemble within the centre arena. Illustration: Eyal Weizman, 2008.

models. Models are like toys – reduced worlds under control. Hartman also thought that the model caused the Israeli jurists 'to recall their youth in military service.'[11] By these means and others it was now the model that was the most important agent in the discussion that followed. As a form of legal document, the model both provided the object of debate and instigated the specific language with which this debate could take place. The procedural change introduced by the model forced and thereby determined the parameters of the discussion. The legal process came to resemble a design session, with the parties making their points on the model, sometimes balancing their pens on its miniature topography to try out alternatives.[12] Legal positions were thus translated into variations in the route of lines, and these routes became diagrams plotting the tensions, debates and force relations. These processes

Parties assemble around the model.
Illustration: Christine Cornell [with Eyal Weizman], 2008.

could later be read by studying the route. As such, Wittgenstein's observation regarding the model is productive to understand the situation at hand: the model presented at court generated the geographical grammar for 'the law' to shape physical reality, in a similar way that a chessboard dictates the possibilities of a game of chess.

Material Proportionality

The ruling was delivered on 30 June 2004. It was based on the court's interpretation of the principle of proportionality. Chief Justice Aharon Barak, who wrote and delivered the verdict, explained that the 'route was

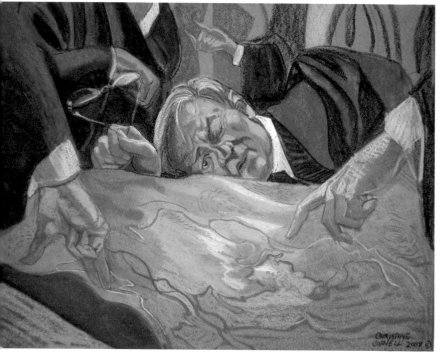

Justice Aharon Barak examines the different routes.
Illustration: Christine Cornell [with Eyal Weizman], 2008.

examined according to a possible alternative that was presented to us'. The judgement, therefore, would be made on whether 'the increased security that is achieved in relation to the alternative presented to us is equivalent against a specific harm done in this case.'[13] The court answered in the negative: the route, it believed, was disproportional to the harm done to the lives of the villagers of Beit Sourik. But what was the proportional line? How many acres of occupied land, litres of olive oil, tonnes of wheat, or hardship or wasted time could be balanced against the optimum visibility from a military vehicle taking a left turn, say? This question will obviously be answered differently by those who drive the vehicle (or who ordered them to do so) and those who cultivate and harvest. In the view of the judges at the High Court, though, the common good of the proposed route accrued to one population – the Israeli Jewish colonizers – and was

Military: *The route drawn by petitioners is unacceptable because it does not take into account the threat to settlements. Placing the fence so close to settlements might put them under constant fire . . . the fence must run on top of the hills to generate topographic surveillance in the valley, as you drew it here, it would be constantly exposed to sniper fire.*

Military: *'Besides the route you proposed is too steep and raises complex engineering problems the fence has roads along it and the route should be no steeper than 6–7 per cent'* Dahla: *'The further the barrier is from the village the safer it is.'*

measured against the lesser evil done to individuals – the Palestinian farmers along the path.

The court seemed to have been convinced that the wall drawn by the Peace and Security Council – the middle line – on Dahla's model was the least harmful one. One of the retired generals of the PSC stated, after 'legal victory' was announced in a subsequent case, that the alternative

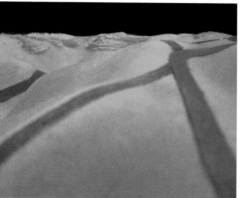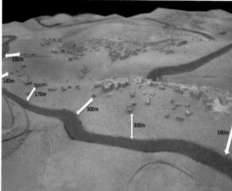

Council for Peace and Security: *The proximity [of the route] to the houses in the Palestinian villages was not only unnecessary from a security perspective but, due to the serious injury to the local population and the consequent friction, actually detrimental to security.'*

route is 'from the point of view of the Palestinian petitioners, the least of all possible evils.'[14] And so it was that the diffused system mediated by the proportionality principle performed the Panglossian function in creating for the Palestinians 'the best of all possible walls'.

The critical legal scholar Aeyal Gross later convincingly explained that the court's interpretation of the principle of proportionality was not in fact adequate. Moreover, he stated, the trial illustrates the way in which the High Court of Jerusalem uses the doctrine of proportionality to legitimize Israel's occupation of the Palestinian territories.[15] Rather than simply acting as retroactive justification of action already perpetrated, the High Court has become an instrument in regulating the occupation by slightly alleviating the worst effects of military violence. Its verdict on the Beit Sourik case was released a few weeks before the International Court of Justice in The Hague published its own advisory opinion. In what Gross called the 'shadow of The Hague on Jerusalem', the HCJ's judgement, and the timing of its announcement, meant to pre-empt that of the International Criminal Court – and in doing so to aid the Israeli state's argument that it applies the rule of law fairly and indifferently in all cases, including those of occupied Palestinians.

The very essence and presence of the wall is the obvious, material embodiment of state ideology and its conception of colonial, territorial and

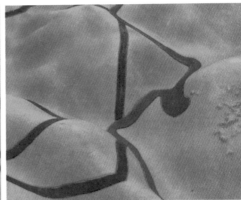

Dahla: *'Given, as you claimed, that the effective range of personal guns is 500 meters, the barrier should be placed further away from the last homes in the villages so as to protect the soldiers patrolling along it.'*

demographic security. It is of course only the most visible element within an assemblage of walls, separated roadways and checkpoints, as well as the invisible web of permit systems, which enact the politics of separation across the entire length and depth of Palestine. The details of the route are, however, not the direct product of top-down government planning. The route's folds, stretches, wrinkles and bends plotted the relative force of different participants brought to bear on it by the different parties and the relative force of their arguments. It is in this context that the wall started appearing as a 'political plastic' – a spatial product made and remade as political forces assume physical form, a diagram of the balance between the forces that shape it. Danny Tirza, the wall's main planner and the representative of the Ministry of Defence in the Beit Sourik trial, called the legally inspired fluctuations of the route 'a political seismograph gone mad'.

Shaped by a legal process, the wall could be said to have been forensically engineered. It has given the principle of proportionality a material and spatial dimension. Material proportionality, then, must be the name of the process by which proportionality analysis helps configure structures and territorial organization. It is the process by which an ethical/legal economy intersects with the science of engineering and the making of things. Through it, the law is mobilized in material action, arranging the distribution of rights across architectural formations and technological systems. Material proportionality gives a new meaning to the concept of security. Security is no longer understood as existing on one side of an equation, on the other side of which sits livelihood and humanitarian issues. Rather, it forms an integrated logic that includes issues like livelihood, human rights and humanitarian concerns within the logic of security. Rather than pitting itself against the agricultural needs of Palestinian farmers, this conception of security aims to embrace and assimilate their concerns over agricultural productivity.

Through the idea of proportionality, differences and disagreements, conflicts and contradictions become 'productive'. In processes concerning proportionality, in which questions of normative moderation arise, the contradictory aims of different actors – military representatives, independent contractors, the media, human rights lawyers, NGOs, social movements and also the victims themselves, those exercising violence and those acting to contain it – add up to a diffused security system that shapes physical reality.

In political terms, the elastic nature of the wall, its capacity to self-modify in response to forces and negotiations, undid the clear conflict and opposition from across a rigid line. The High Court became the arena of negotiations about degrees, measure and balances.

Because the process took place during the high years of the intifada, negotiations shifted from the political realm to the juridical domain, and were conducted not by political representatives, but by lawyers appointed by private villagers. If the wall does ever come to designate the borders of a shrunken temporary Palestinian state, it will be the first such border to have been co-designed by humanitarian lawyers. It is in this way that the Beit Sourik trial provides a reflection on the limits of the process of 'participatory design' – an otherwise banal process based on pseudo-consultation within predefined limits that in this case allowed people to participate in the design of one of the instruments of their most brutal violation, repression and dispossession. And so, case by case, segment by segment, concentrating on problem-solving, moderation and consultation, a major geopolitical question was dismantled and transformed into a humanitarian issue.

Michael Sfard is an Israeli human rights lawyer and one of the most prominent voices of political opposition to Israeli colonialism. He has represented Palestinian landowners in most court cases that followed

A map of the Beit Surik area with the alternative walls drawn on it. Illustration: Bimkom, 2004.

concerning the wall at the High Court of Jerusalem. He explained the nature of his participation in the design and route of the wall like an engineer describing the way a force-field acts on material form:

> The human rights lawyers who petition against the barrier are in fact and in practice one force that designs together with other forces the final route of the wall . . . we find ourselves helping the authorities design a better wall, a wall that goes through a route that is more sustainable. We alert the authorities to the many different problems that the route they designed is causing to livelihood . . . This is the role the army wants me to carry out because it does not know . . . They need me as a go-between to help them create a system that operates better and can last longer. It is very difficult for me to say it but there are several places where I designed the actual route of the wall. It has become clear to me that in fact I am one of its architects.[16]

There is definitively no lack of critical self-awareness in prominent practitioners such as Dahla or Sfard. In fact, most participants in legal struggles against the occupation have reflected, in one way or another, on their collusion with it. In 2007, on the occasion of the occupation's fortieth anniversary, Sfard helped set up a working group of Israeli and Palestinian lawyers, including representatives of most human- and civil rights groups, 'to jointly examine the decades-long struggle against the occupation through petitions to the High Court and other litigation work.' In a situation where the justice system seems to have been enlisted by the defence establishment, they felt it was time for Israeli lawyers to consider alternative forms of action to that of simply petitioning the High Court. Their ideas included connecting local legal struggles to international legal action, boycotts of local courts and a complete shift from technical legalist activism to an overtly political one. These alternatives have yet to be enacted by the participants of the working group – largely because, as they themselves have observed, it would mean 'sacrificing the individuals that seek their help', and might also lead to closing down the organizations they run, which demonstrate the fact that the livelihoods of the Palestinian landowners in the seam area are inversely connected to the livelihoods of the lawyers representing them.

Wallfare

The 'wall' could not, of course, be reduced merely to its physical structure and its route. It is a heterogeneous and interwoven assemblage of interconnected systems of fortification, architectural constructions (the 'terminals'), sensing technologies, automatic weapons, aerial and (in case of Gaza) marine systems that are operated by a multiplicity of institutions according to ever-changing administrative procedures, calculations, tactics, ethical, legal and humanitarian propositions (that capture something of the meaning of what Foucault referred to as 'an apparatus').[17] The organizations that operate the wall participate in the monitoring, control and modulation of everything that passes through it – nutrition, fuel, electricity and medical aid.

While the elastic route of the wall slowly hardens into a definitive form, the permeability of its sister system of fortification, the Gaza perimeter fence, will still be modulated by the proportional mechanisms of the lesser evil. Whereas the case of Beit Sourik dealt with the elasticity of the West Bank wall's route, the following case addresses its permeability: the extent to which it admits essential provisions.

The tightening of the siege of Gaza is the culmination of a process that saw Israel's control of the enclave transformed from a physical 'occupation' – the territorial system of control grounded in a network of military bases, roads and settlements, which was dismantled in the 2005 evacuation – to 'humanitarian management', exercised as the calibration of life-sustaining flows of resources through the physical enclosure, one meant to keep the entire population close to the minimum limit of physical existence.[18]

In September 2007, several weeks after Hamas took control of the Gaza Strip, citing the organization's ongoing rocket fire on Israeli towns, Israel's political-security cabinet declared Gaza a 'hostile entity'. It was a statement that amounted to a declaration of war – short of giving Gaza the status of a state – and outlined Israel's aim: 'to limit the movement of goods into the Gaza Strip, reduce the supply of fuel and electricity, and limit the movement of persons to and from the Strip.' It also described the implementation of a system to regulate and moderate these restrictions. These limitations, the declaration continued, 'will be applied following a legal examination, taking into account the humanitarian situation and with the intention of preventing a humanitarian crisis.'[19] Israel has thus shifted its strategy from trying to hurt Gaza's economy to destroying it altogether and replacing it with a system of humanitarian government. In this it had a participating partner in the Mubarak regime that controlled Egypt's short border with Gaza in Rafah in coordination with Israel's siege.

Although thresholds like that of starvation are scientifically determined by various international organizations and food agencies,[20] the limit of the 'humanitarian minimum' does not exist as a category in international humanitarian law.[21] It was, however, established in a process of juridical adversarial scrutiny, in response to a petition – Case HCJ 9132/07 – submitted on 28 October 2007 to the High Court by Adalah together with eleven other human rights and humanitarian organizations from Israel and Gaza.

The petition protested the siege policy but added, 'even if the closure is meant to serve some appropriate aim, this act could certainly not face the test of proportionality and as such is illegal.' They noted that provisions already fell well short of what the UN said was necessary – a total of 140 megawatts of electricity, 900 truckloads of supplies per week, including 625 loads of foodstuffs and medical supplies, and 275 loads of 'other necessary items' such as personal and home hygiene needs, house cleaning materials and other provisions.[22] The petitioners claimed that there had thus been a humanitarian crisis in Gaza since the early 2000s if not before,[23] and argued that the process of reducing supplies must be stopped and reversed. In response, the Israeli military insisted that the threshold below which 'the residents of the Gaza Strip would be harmed beyond what is necessary' had not yet been breached.[24] For the military, there was still space for further reduction. On a later occasion, when confronted over allegations that the state was deliberately using starvation as a means of collective punishment, the Israeli government press office emailed reporters with copies of the English menu of the restaurant in a Gaza hotel frequented by internationals.[25] It was a travesty as blatant as contesting the severity of the famine in Ethiopia in 1985 based on the menu of the fanciest restaurant in Addis Ababa.

The central task of the legal process was first to define the threshold of the humanitarian minimum, and then find the mechanism to keep to it. In court, military representatives promised that the task of reducing provisions will 'be discharged with the utmost responsibility and seriousness', gradually, and following weekly assessments by experts in security, international law and humanitarianism and electrical engineering. These experts would also maintain 'contacts with UN agencies, international NGOs and Palestinian health officials', who would help determine whether there were 'any indications of a humanitarian crisis developing.' If any signs of such humanitarian crisis were to be detected, the military assured the court that 'the flow of electricity [as of other provisions] will increase.'[26]

The humanitarian minimums were defined in relation to different types of provisions. The team assembling this data for the Ministry of Defense consulted research undertaken in the academy and by the different organizations operating to alleviate famine in relief missions across the world. In the case of nutrition, thresholds were established with the help of physicians and humanitarian nutrition specialists. Another important source for the method of calculating and monitoring provisions in relation to a policy of siege were studies undertaken for the purpose of evaluating the effects of the American-led sanction regime imposed on Iraq after the first Gulf War, which itself was based on calculations of nutrition and medicine.[27] Like the sanctions on Iraq, the siege of Gaza took months to create and perfect and similarly involved a vast network of military and civilian institutions; it was similarly presented as a way of exercising control in its most subtle and cheapest form; and was, most significantly, similarly argued to be an alternative to the far worse scenario of military invasion – we must remember that one of the peace camp's most popular and misguided slogans in the lead-up to the Iraq war was 'Give sanctions a chance', and this regardless of the fact that sanctions led to the death of more than half a million Iraqi children.[28]

The existence of a military document titled *Red Lines* was first revealed in *Ha'aretz* by Yotam Feldman and Uri Blau in June 2009. In October 2010, related files were released in their entirety following a successful freedom-of-information petition submitted by the Israeli NGO Gisha (the Legal Center for Freedom of Movement). The *Red Lines* document outlined the minimum number of calories required to sustain Gaza's population of 1.5 million at a level just above the UN definition of hunger. Using humanitarian standards, officials declared the requirement for adult males to be 2,100 daily calories, females 1,700, and children variable amounts, depending on gender and age. They calculated the foodstuffs produced in Gaza and the number of people in the strip. The total number of calories arrived at was then divided into cereals, fruits and vegetables, meat, milk and oil. These in turn were translated into tonnage and the number of trucks of international agencies – Israel would not finance these deliveries – to be allowed into Gaza. Dov Weisglass, adviser to Prime Minister Ehud Olmert, explained the rationale: 'The idea is to put the Palestinians on a diet, but not to make them die of hunger.'[29] According to a constantly shifting scale, certain foodstuffs were defined as 'essential', such as persimmons, bananas and apples – and, usually, whatever unsold stocks Israeli wholesalers were stuck with at any given time. Other foodstuffs considered 'luxury' – such as apricots, plums, avocados and grapes – were forbidden.[30]

Baruch Spiegel, a reserve general in the Israeli military, best embodies Israel's attempts to govern the strip by 'managing' the humanitarian situation as an instrument of state policy. His career in recent years encapsulates Israel's strategic transition from a territorial system of domination to humanitarian government. Previously, Spiegel headed up a team dealing with 'civilian and humanitarian issues caused by the wall and checkpoints' in the West Bank. He worked closely with Palestinian and Israeli NGOs and international organizations in their efforts to reroute the wall or to open what the military called 'humanitarian gates'. Since Dahla's team secured the 'legal defeat' of the state in the Beit Surik case, his work saved the military much time and money, avoiding lengthy and costly legal processes, as he was in charge of enacting alternatives to the route in out-of-court settlements. Spiegel's next posting, to which he was appointed during the 2008–9 attack in Gaza, was as head of a makeshift 'humanitarian war room' located in one of the terminals on the Gaza perimeter. The war room was a meeting place for Israeli military officers and humanitarian agents, among them UN agencies such as UNRWA (UN Relief and Work Association, which deals with Palestinian refugees), WFO (World Food Organization) and WHO (World Health Organization), the ICRC, USAID and occasionally representatives of the EU and of various international NGOs. The forum's task was, of course, to solve the humanitarian problems created as a result of the inability to transfer even a minimum of humanitarian provisions under fire, to determine need and crisis and responses to them. Spiegel explained, 'The model of a combined humanitarian centre reflected shared interest and understanding . . . It was very helpful for the IDF, Israel and the international agencies.'[31]

The siege was in fact a military operation that relied on endless daily calculations, themselves modified in relation to the constant monitoring of the situation in Gaza as reported by international organizations. Numerical formulas with upper and lower thresholds defined what the military called the 'breathing space' – which is to say the time left before hunger starts killing people. In the *Red Lines* documents uncovered by Gisha, the military orders for calculating food provision were defined by the following formulae, meant for those managing the crossing, and reminiscent of primary school algebra lessons.

If the daily consumption per capita, per product as calculated by the Palestinian Central Bureau of Statistics is A, the population of the Gaza Strip is B, then daily consumption C should be calculated as $C = A*B$.

If the quantity of food reserves in the Gaza Strip is Z, the breathing space in days [D] should be calculated as $D = Z/C$.

If the daily quantity of produce entering the Gaza Strip is X and the existing reserves in the Gaza Strip is Y, the quantity of reserves in the Gaza Strip should be calculated as $Z = X+Y-C$

In simple language: if you divide food in the Strip by the daily consumption needs of residents, you will get the number of days it will take before people run out of basic provisions and start dying.

The Israeli theorist Ariella Azoulay explained in 2003 that although it has brought the Occupied Territories to the verge of hunger, the Israeli government tries to control the flow of provisions in such a way as to prevent the situation from reaching a point of total collapse, all because of the unpredictable international reaction that might follow.[32] Similarly, the scholar and human rights researcher Darryl Li points out that the term 'disengagement' – usually used to refer to the Sharon government's 2005 withdrawal from the colonies in Gaza – should rather be used to refer to a new type of regime of controlled abandonment. 'Disengagement', writes Li, 'is a form of rule that sets as its goal neither justice nor even stability, but rather survival – as we are reminded by every guarantee that an undefined "humanitarian crisis" will be avoided.'[33] Adi Ophir describes Israel's policy towards Gaza as 'catastrophization': 'When catastrophization becomes a set of governmental policies, a measured and restrained means of governance, the presence of an imaginary, ghost-like threshold of catastrophe often becomes a warning sign ... These forces should not cross the imaginary line lest they lose the legitimization of those who support them [in order] to keep the catastrophe itself in suspension.'[34] In an article expanding on his journalistic account of the *Red Lines* documents, Yotam Feldman refers to the rationing of calories into Gaza as 'the ethic of red-lines,' an operational mode which, he explains, 'allows the security forces to undertake all action as long as this line is not breached.'[35]

However, the elasticity of such thresholds means that in reality not much is held in suspense. Rather than the red line functioning as a minimum threshold with the level of provisions fluctuating over it, at the moment it was accepted by the high court, the line began designating the maximum cap on provisions. Although the military ceaselessly propagates the idea that it monitors and adheres to the humanitarian minimums, at no point did it provide the same amount or more electricity, medical aid and nutrition than the minimum to which it was committed. Moreover, in a downward spiral, every time a new lowest level was recorded, it immediately became the benchmark to define a new 'normal state' against which further reductions could be implemented as punishment. The siege reached a stage where widespread hunger could be held at bay only by the constant and audacious operations that imported food from Sinai through the hundreds of supply tunnels dug under the Egyptian border.

Furthermore, the tragedy of Gaza cannot be wholly evaluated by the number of recorded deaths from violent reasons or from causes related to hunger. Rather, it needs to factor a slower, more cumulative process in which deaths that might have been averted were actively not prevented. Relative to other conflicts worldwide, the Israel–Palestine one does not produce a high number of direct or violent deaths, while those deaths that do take place are relatively visible.[36] But another, rather more subtle form of killing has become commonplace: one that is undertaken through degrading environmental conditions to affect the quality of water, hygiene, nutrition and healthcare; by restricting the flow of life-sustaining infrastructure, forbidding the importation of water purifiers and much-needed vitamins (mainly B12), by restrictions on planning and by making it difficult for patients to travel. This form of killing – almost Malthusian in its conception – deliberately sought to control the living conditions, and is part of current Israeli policy in relation to Gaza. Figures of 'excess mortality' – those related to avoidable death that have not been avoided or intentionally allowed – are difficult to establish; they are buried in comparative statistical calculations of trends in mortality rates. This might also account for the reason that indirect mortality rates have rarely been used, not even by those mobilizing world opinion against all forms of Israeli domination.[37]

Milgram in Gaza

The legal petition against the further reduction of provisions into Gaza was rejected at the end of January 2008. 'This is the difference between Israel, a democracy fighting for its life within the framework of the law, and the terrorist organizations fighting against it,' the High Court stated, as if it were a state spokesperson. The court performed the task of an administrator rather than an adjudicator, a partner in the calibration of how much pain Gazans are to be made to legitimately feel. As such, acts of torture and terror aimed at forcing civilians into political compliance conferred on their makers a dignified image. Those proportionaly administering the level of pain could now see themselves as being responsible for the necessary and tragic task of calculating and responsibly choosing the lesser of all possible evils.

Unlike other provisions, imported through the hundreds of tunnels between Egypt and Gaza, which threw out Israel's modulations and calculations, Israel has complete control over the supply of electricity. Examining the fluctuations of electrical current therefore yields a revealing picture of how Israel forced the designated thresholds to the breaking point.

The ability to exercise control through the modulation of flow – in which the checkpoints and terminals within the wall function as valves and switches – has made Israel's warfare on Gaza resemble an inverse Milgram experiment. In reflecting upon the willing participation of individuals in the functioning of repressive regimes, the Yale professor Stanley Milgram's infamous 1961 experiment sought to investigate the extent to which ordinary people would obey the orders of figures in authority to inflict pain on others. On one side of a room divided by a one-way mirror, a scientist ordered a volunteer to deliver electrical shocks of ever-increasing strength to a person strapped to a chair on the other side of the room whenever she or he gave wrong answers to questions read from a questionnaire. In the experiment, the person answering the questions was an actor: there was no current in the system and the effects of the shocks were simulated. Those administering the 'shocks' were, unknowingly, the subjects of an experiment in the limits of their obedience to a figure of scientific authority. Most were willing to inflict pain beyond the threshold marked as life endangering, when ordered to do so.

An analogous process happened in the context of administering the siege of Gaza, with the crucial difference that the current in Gaza was real enough and the response to bad political choices by the Hamas government was not to increase the current but rather to reduce it gradually – and thereby destroy the strip's life-sustaining infrastructure and eventually bring its population to the brink of physical existence. In this inverted

Milgram experiment, the authority figures are the scientists, engineers and humanitarian experts advising the Israeli High Court, which ultimately decides on the level of current. Although those administering the reduction guarantee to provide current at a threshold above that at which a 'humanitarian crisis will be created', this threshold was constantly tested – much like the upper limits of the electric shock in the Milgram experiment.

Nearly all of Gaza's energy is supplied by Israel, both directly, from its electric grid, paid for by tax revenues collected by Israel on behalf of the Palestinian National Authority (PNA), and indirectly, through fuel supplies paid for by the European Union and supplied by the Israeli company Dor Alon to Gaza's only electrical power plant. Nine high-voltage power lines from Israel and one from Egypt supply Gaza with a maximum of about 140 megawatts (MW). From 2 February 2008 – days after the legal judgment on the humanitarian minimum – the military reduced the current supplied by each of the power lines in turn by 5 per cent every week for the next several months.[38] Another 140 MW were provided by the Gaza Power Plant, a structure built by Enron and which opened a few weeks after the company's collapse at the end of 2001. Israel reduced the power plant's capacity by gradually reducing the supply of industrial diesel. The power plant requires a supply of 3.5 million litres of industrial diesel weekly to work at its full capacity. The high court accepted as the humanitarian minimum a quota of 2.2 million, which would reduce its operation to about 68 per cent of capacity. At this level the Gaza Electricity Company had to initiate regular blackouts, and spread the burden of the power outages over the different distribution areas of each power line in order to keep hospitals and other vital services running.

On 9 April 2008, two Israeli citizens were killed by militants at an Israeli-controlled border crossing where this very industrial diesel is piped into Gaza. Israel saw this as ingratitude for the minimum level of fuel provided, and a Ministry of Defence spokesperson declared that from that point on, the opening of the crossings 'will be evaluated on a day to day basis'. Israel immediately reduced the flow of diesel to 1.5 million litres per week, 42 per cent of what was required for the Gaza Power Plant's full capacity, and 24 per cent below the threshold of the legally defined red line. Electricity production dropped to 45 MW. Power cuts now affected fresh water pumping from the coastal aquifer, thereby aggravating the water shortages. Crop irrigation was interrupted, destroying fruit and fodder production, which in turn reduced egg and dairy output. When the current was further reduced, fish started dying in the Beit Lahiya fish farms because the pumps needed to filter or oxygenate water stopped functioning. Sewage pumping also decreased. In some cisterns the level of sewage rose to the point where the concrete banks of container pools collapsed. Raw sewage started flooding onto streets and agricultural fields, seeping into the aquifer's drinking water. In May 2008 the sewage treatment plant overflowed: more than 50 million litres of raw waste poured into the Mediterranean every day, further affecting public health and reducing the fishing catches. Slowly, it also started affecting Israeli beaches. Israeli coastal municipalities north of Gaza started complaining, asking for more current to be supplied to Gaza. In June 2008 Israel increased the flow of diesel close to the level of the 'humanitarian minimum', allowing the power station to reach 60 MW again and for the sewage farms to be repaired and restarted. Depending on the political calculation at any given time, the military reduced or increased the supply of diesel, seeking to achieve an optimum of maximum political impact with minimum intervention. Although there were small demonstrations against Hamas' rule during times of drastic reduction, Hamas' control of Gaza was generally strengthened during this period due to the fact that it was the only supplier of emergency services.

When, on 5 November 2008, after Israeli forces killed six Hamas gunmen in a raid into the territory, breaking the ceasefire that had held for several months, all diesel supply to Gaza was swiftly cut off, together with all other provisions. On 5 November the Israeli government sealed every way into and out of Gaza. Egypt did the same on its border to the strip.[39] On 5 November the capacity of the power plant went to 18 per cent of the 'humanitarian minimum', but then supplies dried up again and the entire plant shut down three days later. When a single fuel truck arrived on 18 November, the turbine batteries failed to start up, and the plant's engineers worked frantically to hook up 170 twelve-volt car batteries from cars in the plant parking lot to restart the plant's turbines. They succeeded but the plant soon shut down again for lack of diesel. For half the days in November and December, the plant was unable to produce any electricity whatsoever. Overstretched generators collapsed. In hospitals, computers and medical equipment fell into disuse. Surgeries and medical lab services were cancelled. Refrigeration outages rendered stockpiles of drugs useless; even the morgues shut down. Just as it seemed things could not get any worse, on 27 December the first bombs started falling. But considering Israel's more invisible and lesser-known humanitarian attack – exercised across the wall of Gaza – the war of 2008–9 was all over before it had even begun.

A Legislative Attack

> If, therefore, conclusions can be drawn from military violence, as being primordial and paradigmatic of all violence used for natural ends, there is inherent in all such violence a lawmaking character.[40]
>
> Walter Benjamin

Israel's bombing and invasion of Gaza in the winter of 2008–9 marked the culmination of its violence against the Palestinians since the Nakba of 1948, and resulted in widespread international allegations that Israel had committed war crimes. It was also the assault with which Israeli experts in international humanitarian law – the area of the law that regulates the conduct of war – had their closest involvement to date. Since the 2006 Lebanon War the Israeli military has become increasingly mindful about its exposure to international legal action. Preparations for the next conflict included those in the domain of law, and new 'legal technologies' were introduced in military matters.

This development gives rise to a series of related questions. Might it be that these legal technologies contributed not to the containment of violence but to its proliferation? That the involvement of military lawyers did not in fact restrain the attack – but rather, that certain interpretations of international humanitarian law have enabled the inflicting of unprecedented levels of destruction? In other words, has the making of this chaos, death and destruction been facilitated by the terrible force of the law?

*   *   *

In more domains than one, the elastic and porous border has become the contemporary pathology of Israel's regime of control. It manifests itself in a variety of different ways – one such being the elasticity that military lawyers identify and mobilize in interpreting the laws of war.

The laws of war pose a paradox to those protesting in their name: while they prohibit some things, they authorize others. And thus another borderline is established between the 'allowed' and the 'forbidden'. This line is not stable and static, rather it is dynamic and elastic and its path is ever changing. An intense battle is conducted over its route. Much like the route of the separation wall, the thresholds of the law will be pulled and pushed in different directions by those with different objectives. The question hinges on which side of the legal/illegal divide a certain form of military practice is to be located. International organizations such as the UN and the ICRC, large NGOs and human rights groups, and also some highly regarded academic authorities on international humanitarian law, have the means to push the line in one direction – to place controversial military practices on the prohibited side – while state militaries and their apologists seek to push it in the opposite direction. International law can thus not be thought of as a static body of rules but rather an arena in which the law is shaped by an endless series of diffused border conflicts.

According to the legal scholar and adviser for the ICRC in Israel Eitan Diamond, 'the architecture of international humanitarian law is typified by "rigid lines of absolute prohibition" and "elastic zones of discretion."' The rigid prohibitions are derived, he states, from the law's origins in the nineteenth century, 'a time when legal thought was dominated by a positivist-formalist approach that conceived of law as a closed system distinguished from politics and ethics'. Today, he fears, 'states and their advocates are using arguments based on the logic of the "lesser evil" to subvert the law's absolute provisions and to subject them to malleable cost-benefit calculations.'[41] Diamond and the ICRC – allergic to the 'creativity' of state lawyers – would prefer to see a more rigid legal structure and absolute prohibitions. A deontological legal system demanding the strict application of the law is useful in the kind of backroom discussions the ICRC is involved in with the military.

New frontiers of military practice are being explored via a combination of legal technologies and complex institutional practices that are now often referred to as 'lawfare', the use of law as a weapon of war. Lawfare is a compounded practice: with the introduction and popularization of international law in contemporary battlefields, all parties to a conflict might seek to use it for their tactical and strategic advantage. The former American colonel and military judge Charles Dunlap, who was credited with the introduction of this term in 2001, suggested that 'lawfare' can be defined as 'the strategy of using – or misusing – law as a substitute for traditional military means to achieve an operational objective.'[42] In the hands of non-state actors, Dunlap says, the 'lawfare effect' is created by an interaction between guerrilla groups that 'lure militaries to conduct atrocities' and human rights groups that engage in advocacy to expose these atrocities, and who use what available means for litigation they have to hand. In a similar vein, Israel now often claims that it is facing an unprecedented campaign of lawfare, which threatens to undermine the very legitimacy of the state. Lawfare is also used tactically by state militaries themselves. In this context it refers to the multiple ways by which contemporary warfare is conditioned, rather than simply justified, by international law.[43] In both cases, international law and the systems of courts and tribunals that exercise and enact it are not conceived as spaces outside the conflict, but rather as being among the battlegrounds internal to it.

Anarchists Against the Law

It is within the 'elastic zones of discretion' that Israeli military lawyers find enormous potential for the expansion of military action. A former chief international lawyer for the Israeli military, Daniel Reisner, argued that because international humanitarian law is not so much a code-based legal system but a precedent-based legal corpus, state practice can continuously shift it.

> International law is a customary law that develops through an historic process. If states are involved in a certain type of military activity against other states, militias, and the like, and if all of them act quite similarly to each other, then there is a chance that it will become customary international law.[44]

It is in this sense that international law develops through its violation. In modern war *violence legislates*: 'If the same process occurred in criminal law, the legal speed limit would be 115 kilometres an hour and income tax would be 4 per cent.'[45]

Reisner is proud to have been the first international lawyer to have defended, at a specific request of then–prime minister Ehud Barak, the policy of 'targeted assassinations' towards the end of 2000, when most governments and international bodies considered the practice illegal. 'We invented the targeted assassination thesis and we had to push it. At first there were protrusions that made it hard to insert easily into the legal moulds. Eight years [and, as he said subsequently in this interview, referring to 9/11, "four planes"] later it is in the centre of the bounds of legitimacy.'[46]

Asa Kasher, a professor of ethics at Tel Aviv University, has worked with Reisner to provide an ethical and legal defence for targeted assassination. He talks in similar terms about the nature of law and the ways in which it might be transformed: 'We in Israel have a crucial part to play in the developing of this area of the law [international humanitarian law] because we are at the forefront of the war against terror, and [the tactics we use] are gradually becoming acceptable in Israeli and in international courts of law . . . The more often Western states apply principles that originated in Israel to their own non-traditional conflicts in places like Afghanistan and Iraq, then the greater the chance these principles have of becoming a valuable part of international law. What we *do* becomes the law.'[47]

After the Goldstone fact-finding mission on Gaza, Israel's prime minister emphatically called for a radical rewriting of international humanitarian law. 'Paradoxically,' Benjamin Netanyahu said, 'it is possible that the firm response of important international leaders and jurists to [the Goldstone report] will accelerate the re-examination of the laws of war in an age of terror.' His Minister of Defence, Ehud Barak, added: 'We cannot change the law but we can help develop it.'

The actions of the Israeli state against Gaza may become acceptable in law. The siege, ongoing since 2007, the 2008–9 invasion, and the 2009 attack on an international flotilla carrying supplies into the enclave, have all been carried out with relative impunity, and do not appear to have significantly affected Israel's international standing. Each of these forms of aggression contains within it a multiplicity of small-scale practices and incidents: restricting the supply of food to the threshold of starvation; targeted assassinations; sending advance warnings that then allow the military to kill those civilians who choose not to evacuate;[48] attacks on activists in international waters; the use of white phosphorus in inhabited areas – the list goes on. In these acts – if Israeli lawyers have their way and continue to play with the law as if it was a toy – lie the seeds of new legislation.

Working on the margins of the law is one way to expand them. For violence to have the power to legislate it needs to be applied in the grey, indeterminate zone between obvious violation and possible legality, and then to be defended diplomatically and by legal opinion. Indeed, the legal tactics sanctioned by military lawyers in Israel's invasion of Gaza in 2008–9 were framed in precisely this way. 'When something's in the white zone, I'll let it be done, if it's in the black I'll forbid it, but if it's in the grey zone then I'll take part in the dilemma, I don't stop at grey,' said Reisner. Proportionality might indeed be thought of as one of the mechanisms for the reshaping of juridical space in a way that increases the extent of and makes use of the grey zone.

The invasion therefore did two simultaneous and seemingly paradoxical things: it both violated the law and aimed to shift its thresholds. This kind of violence not only transgresses but also attacks the very idea of rigid limits. In this circular logic, the illegal turns legal through continuous violation. There is indeed a 'law making character' inherent in military violence. This is law in action, legislative violence as seen from the perspective of those who write it in practice.

This use of the law has much in common with that of the George W. Bush administration's misappropriation of the Office of Special Counsel in the Justice Department, in order to figure out a way to legalize the use of torture. Inherent in this was the clear intention to stretch the law as far as possible without actually breaking it.[49] In this example, US Department of Justice Attorney John Yoo used balancing of interests to authorize certain forms of torture. His famous torture memos were grounded in an Israeli precedent: relying on what is essentially a proportionality analysis, the 1987 Israeli commission of inquiry into the methods of investigation in the General Security Service (the Landau Commission) arrived at the conclusion that the prohibition on torture is not absolute, but is rather based, using the commission's words, 'upon the logic of the lesser evil'.

Thus, 'the harm done by violating a provision of the law during an interrogation must be weighed against the harm to the life or person of others which could occur sooner or later'.[50] Some legal scholars have suggested that such legal advice in itself might be considered a crime.

Similar lines of legal argument are inspired by a strand of legal scholarship known as 'critical legal studies', an approach that emerged together with other post-structuralist discourses at the end of the 1980s. Critical legal studies scholars aimed to expose the way the law is made, the workings of power in the making and enactment of law, to challenge law's normative account and to offer an insight into its internal contradictions and indeterminacies. It was, broadly speaking, a critical, left-leaning practice, which otherwise attempted to deploy law at the service of a socially transformative agenda. But when international law stands as an obstacle in the way of state militaries it is easy to see why military lawyers would adopt the attitude of those scholars seeking to challenge rigid definitions and expose the law as an object of critique and contestation. Today, when the creative interpretation of the law is exercised by state and military lawyers, it is primarily human rights and anti-war activists that insist on the dry letter of the law. This creative treatment of the law, as exercised by the military and its advocates, led Michael Sfard to play on the phrase 'anarchists against the wall' – a group of anti-occupation activists – to describe Israeli military lawyers as 'anarchists against the law'.[51]

The appeal, by military lawyers, to international humanitarian law to justify wars could easily be dismissed as cynical propaganda. Most human rights groups have correctly pointed out that international humanitarian law was not properly observed in Gaza, in the sense that it was used too permissively. Evidence and testimonies, including soldiers', collected by the Goldstone investigation and human rights groups reveal in baroquely nightmarish details some of the most gruesome and egregious violations. There were about twenty reported instances of Israeli soldiers firing at women and children carrying white flags; reports of the denial of medical aid and ambulances to reach wounded Palestinians who bled to death; the wanton destruction of homes and neighbourhoods; and the use of white phosphorus – and more besides.[52] But in the age of lawfare, the elastic nature of the law, and the power of military action to stretch it, those appealing for justice in the name of the law need to be aware of its double edge.

Gaza is a laboratory in more than one sense. It is a hermetically sealed zone, with all access controlled by Israel (except the Egypt border, now controlled by a still yet-to-be-defined post-Mubarak regime). Within this enclosed space, all sorts of new control technologies, munitions, legal and humanitarian tools, and warfare techniques are tried out on its million and a half inhabitants. The ability to remotely control large populations is also tested, before these technologies are marketed internationally. Most significantly of all, it is the thresholds that are tested and pushed: the limits of the law, and the limits of violence that can be inflicted by a state and be internationally tolerated. This limit, newly defined with every attack, will become the new threshold of what can be done to people in the name of 'war on terror'. When the legislative violence directed at Gaza unlocks the chaotic powers of destruction that lie dormant within the law, the consequence will be felt by oppressed people everywhere.

Marc Garlasco speaking at Bard College's Human Rights Project (HRP) about violations of the laws of war in the Gaza offensive of 2008–9. Photograph courtesy of HRP, 2010.

4

Forensic Architecture:
Only the Criminal Can Solve the Crime

> The love of ruins has generated various epistemes and disciplines: In the
> sixteenth century it informed philology, in the nineteenth century histori-
> ography and criminology . . . [now] the physis of the fragments took the
> place of virtual debris and the love of ruins became a fetish.[1]
>
> Cornelia Vismann 'The Love of Ruins'

A strange story unfolded in the shadows of the legal and diplomatic furore
that accompanied the release, on 15 September 2009, of Richard
Goldstone's 'Report of the United Nations Fact Finding Mission on the
Gaza Conflict'. The report alleged that both the Israeli military and Hamas
had committed war crimes, and indeed that Israel might even be guilty of
'crimes against humanity'.[2] On the same day, Human Rights Watch
(HRW), still in the process of conducting its own in-depth analysis of
Israel's invasion of Gaza in early 2009, announced the suspension of its
'senior military analyst' and 'expert on battle damage assessment' Marc
Garlasco. Garlasco had joined HRW's 'emergencies division' in 2003 after
seven years as an intelligence analyst in the US Defense Intelligence
Agency, where he was a 'targeting' and 'battle damage assessment' expert.
During NATO's attack in Kosovo and Serbia and the subsequent US-led
attack on Iraq, Garlasco had been involved in selecting bombing targets
and the munitions for their destruction, and also in the 'proportionality
assessment' that designated the maximum number of civilian deaths for
bombing missions to comply with international humanitarian law.

Crucially, these military tasks meant that he had to familiarize himself with the structure and construction techniques of buildings and with the way they collapse, a skill that was later of use in his role as Human Rights Watch's in-house forensic expert in charge of examining battle damage. At HRW his investigations had focused largely on the examination of material remains – building rubble and shrapnel – found in the aftermath of attacks, and on military technology used. Providing crucial material evidence and expert analysis for HRW's research on violations of IHL and human rights in Iraq, Afghanistan, Lebanon, Gaza, Myanmar and Georgia,[3] he built up a considerable professional reputation, a media presence, and quite a few detractors (mainly with those human rights people that did not like a former soldier in their midst, but also those against which he wrote) , and, by the time of his suspension, had authored and contributed to a series of reports alleging violations of international humanitarian law by the Israeli military, in both its Gaza offensive and a string of earlier incidents.[4] In the Goldstone report, the reports he worked on were cited on thirty-six occasions.

Some 1,400 people were killed and 15,000 buildings destroyed or damaged in the Gaza attack of December 2008–January 2009.[5] There is, unsurprisingly, a correlation between these figures: a large proportion of the deaths occurred within buildings. Indeed, many individuals and families were killed by flying debris – the shattered concrete and glass of what used to be the walls, ceilings and windows of their own homes. One person I called in Gaza during the attack spoke of 'buildings turning from solid structures to dust, and the dust of homes filling the air . . . people breathing in pulverized building parts.' The built environment became more than just a target or battleground; it was turned into the very things that killed. When on 18 January 2009 the bombing ended and the dust finally settled, the way it settled now became evidence. Allegations about the Israeli military's deliberate destruction of homes and infrastructure were made – and contested – using geospatial data, satellite imagery of destroyed buildings and data gathered in on-site investigations. Much of this research was concerned with the 'interrogation' of the ruins and rubble of destroyed buildings, a process to which Garlasco's expertise made a significant contribution. The emphasis on the investigation of material remains and their overwhelming abundance meant that the forensic analysis of built structures – a practice I would like to refer to as 'forensic architecture' – emerged at the forefront of the legal–political disputes that ensued.

Existing at the intersection of architecture, history and the laws of war, forensic architecture must refer to an analytical method for reconstructing scenes of violence as they are inscribed in spatial artefacts and in built environments. The facts of destruction were of course all evident: it was abundantly clear to anyone following the war who had caused the destruction, and in which context. The investigation was not overtly political so much as technical. The commission employing international forensics experts explored heaps of rubble in order to gather information about how an event unfolded and whether, by extension, it was legal or illegal under international humanitarian law. However, the ferocity of the debate in this instance meant that not only the forensic analyses but the analysts themselves came under prolonged scrutiny. Marc Garlasco was a case in point.

Garlasco's September 2009 suspension was Human Rights Watch's response to a controversy that had been precipitated by a single blog posting, with a deluge of further blogs following suit, 'revealing' that he was a collector of Nazi-era memorabilia, that he had authored a book on Nazi-era military medals and had reviewed others on the subject, that he is a regular contributor to several internet collector forums and has expressed unreserved enthusiasm for – and some macabre humour apropos of – Nazi-era memorabilia.[6] They called this obsession fetishism and went on to demand his disqualification.

People involved in the analysis of war scenes tend to have a certain obsession with the objects of war. But pro-Israeli organizations, and spokespeople for the Israeli government itself, claimed Garlasco's enthusiasms distorted his capacity for impartial analysis in matters pertaining to Israel. For pro-Israeli spokespersons the revelation regarding Garlasco's interests was a gift, as it could help demonstrate what they had long claimed to be a far more widespread and deep-rooted bias against Israel among human rights organizations, even, perhaps, constituting the ultimate validation of the general claim that the state's detractors – now armed with the legal tools of human rights and humanitarian law – are driven by anti-Semitism and are set on delegitimizing the Jewish state. For them, the discourse around human rights has thus come full circle – a sensibility and an ethics of compassion grounded in the identification with victims, the Jewish victims of the Holocaust being its prime reference – has been universalized to become a new weapon in the ever-renewing arsenal of anti-Semitism.

In a November 2009 lecture at the Saban Forum, one of Israel's leading security studies institutes, Prime Minister Benjamin Netanyahu identified three strategic threats facing Israel.[7] After naming 'a nuclear Iran' and 'missile and rocket attacks' from Hamas and Hezbollah, he went on to say that the third threat comprised 'attempts to deny Israel the right to self-defence. The UN Goldstone report on Gaza attempts to do that.' Organizations mobilizing to support human rights principles and international law then emerged as a strategic threat on par with Hezbollah and Iran.[8] Then Netanyahu announced his government's decision to 'combat' the Goldstone report and the lawfare undertaken in its name. A few weeks previously, Ron Dermer, Netanyahu's policy director, who had threatened to 'fight back' against the 'attempts by human rights groups to delegitimize Israel', explained that state officials would 'dedicate time and manpower to combating these groups'. Dermer then seized on the Garlasco revelations, calling the forensics expert's interest in Nazi memorabilia 'a new low'.[9]

In heightening the significance of this controversy, Israel managed to deflect some attention from its actions in Gaza and elsewhere. But Garlasco's story, which meanwhile was drowned in the deluge of other controversies and events, is important for other reasons. In particular, it can help us reflect upon the emergent practice of forensic architecture and indeed on the function and significance of forensics as recently employed in the service of 'international justice'. Rather than illustrating a certain ingrained bias against Israel, I would propose that Garlasco's story offers a glimpse into the growing proximity between human rights organizations and the militaries of Western states, Israel's included. This proximity is expressed by a shared language, sometimes overlapping aims and a fluid exchange of personnel. It is a proximity without which the Garlasco affair could not have unfolded.

In order, then, to have this event shed new light on the politics of war-crime investigations, the story of Garlasco and that of forensic architecture will proceed along two entangled narrative arcs in what follows. The first will trace the development of a recent epistemic shift in international law, in which an emphasis on forensic practices has been pronounced. The second will look at Marc Garlasco's career path from the Pentagon to the changing world of human rights, as a registration of the latter's ever closer proximity to violence. The controversy that occurred in 2009, around the accusation of fetishism, was the result of an inevitable collision between these two trajectories.

Before the Forum

In discussing its approach to the investigation of war crimes, the 'methodology' section of the Goldstone report reveals a slight – yet significant – shift of emphasis from human testimony to material evidence. While the report included dozens of testimonies from witnesses, it also assumed that the reliability of those witness statements would be keenly contested. The report, therefore, tips the balance towards objects and objectivity. 'The Mission conducted field visits, including investigations of incident sites,' it stated. The investigations reviewed 10,000 documents and used 'analysis of video and photographic images . . . satellite photographs [1,200 in total], and expert analysis of such images, medical reports . . . weapons and ammunition remnants . . . [and interpreted these findings in] meetings with military analysts, medical doctors, legal experts, scientists, etc.'[10]

This shift is interesting because Richard Goldstone, the report's author, formerly a liberal apartheid judge and a chief prosecutor in the international tribunals for the former Yugoslavia (ICTY) and Rwanda (ICTR), was also one of the promoters and defenders of the South African 'truth and reconciliation committees' – the process most identified with oral testimony, with story-telling and the subjective interpretation of 'witnesses', 'perpetrators' and 'victims'.[11] The shift of emphasis from human testimony towards objects of material evidence and forensics in this investigation is indicative of larger cultural and political transformations – indeed a certain 'forensic fetishism' that needs to be unpacked.

The assumption that underpins forensic analysis of this kind is that,

Richard Goldstone's press conference in Gaza, 2009.
Photograph AP: This image is perhaps one of the best demonstrations of the contemporary principle of forensics. Goldstone stands in front of a destroyed multi-storied building. Around him are members of the government in Gaza; before him is a bouquet of microphones belonging to international news networks. Since the ruined building can not speak for itself, Goldstone seems to have taken on the task of speaking on its behalf, interpreting the story of the building to an international forum.

unlike the testimony of victims, scientific evidence pronounced by expert witnesses is more difficult to contest; that bullets and missile casings, ruins, medical and autopsy reports and tissues showing the burn mark of white phosphorus presumably cannot be undermined by any suspect political subjectivity – which is what some experts in international law seem to think the people of Gaza indulge in, or they are concerned that others might think this to be the case. Presentations of the report were thus reinforced by clichés of the kind that often give evidence an almost human status. 'Evidence speaks for itself,' albeit unlike humans, 'it does not lie'. The difference between testimony and evidence, and thus between people and objects, is that subjects can misremember or skew their testimony in relation to their political self-interest while an evidentiary truth seems to linger, fossilized in the object, ready to be unpacked by science. The rubble of destroyed buildings can thus not be pro-Israeli or pro-Hamas, or pronounced as skewed evidence on behalf of either. The history of forensics, might, however, demonstrate that investigating and presenting such evidence involves arduous construction conducted with the aid of scientific protocols, rhetoric, theatrics and the professional and ethical credibility necessary to construct indisputable facts; that in the interpretation of the object some of the problems associated with the witness are reproduced. These investigations must also include a certain indispensable passion for the object, which would later be discussed in relation to the controversy around forensic fetishism.

The history of jurisprudence tells of a constant tension between human testimony and material evidence, and an ongoing shift of emphasis, at different periods, between them. Derived from the Latin *forensis*, the word's root refers to the 'forum', and the practice and skill of making an argument before a professional, political or legal gathering. In classical Rome forensics was part of rhetoric, which of course concerns speech. However, forensics included not only human speech but also that of objects. In forensic rhetoric, objects could address the forum. Because objects do not speak for themselves, there is a need for 'translation' or 'interpretation' – forensic rhetoric requires a person (or a set of technologies) to mediate between the object and the forum: to present the object, interpret it and place it within a larger narrative. This was the role of the rhetoricians and today is the role of the expert witness. Forensics is the way objects appear and are debated in the forum, with the forum being the arena of interpretation where claims and counter-claims have to be made.

The principle of forensics assumes two interrelated sets of spatial relations. The first is the relation between an event and the object in which traces of that event are registered. The second is a relation between the object and the forum that assembles around it and to which its 'speech' is addressed. Forensics is therefore as concerned with the materialization of the event as with the construction of a forum and the performance of objects and interpreters within it. The forums to which contemporary forensics are addressed are not, however, the actual spaces of the court; they are often contingent, diffused and networked, created through and by the media, assembled around found evidence, and operate across a multiplicity of international institutions. Within them, the object and its 'interpreter' constitute a single rhetorical unit. To refute a forensic statement it is necessary to dismantle the mechanisms of its articulation, which means to show that the object is inauthentic, that its interpreter is biased or that the communication between them is short-circuited. All the above techniques were employed against Goldstone and Garlasco in their research on Gaza. Garlasco, furthermore, was not only accused of misinterpreting objects, but of being nothing less than possessed by them.

There is much that relates to fetishism about forensics – where objects are asked to speak. The Roman orators referred to speech on behalf of inanimate objects as *prosopopoeia*: a rhetorical technique that artificially endows inanimate objects with a voice. In discussing 'giving a voice to things to which nature has not given a voice', the rhetorician Quintilian writes of the power of *prosopopoeia* to 'bring down the gods from heaven, evoke the dead, and give voices to cities and states.'[12] Forensic specialists and expert witnesses are very fond of using figures of speech in which 'the evidence', 'the rubble' or 'the bones' – in the case of mass exhumations – are 'speaking to us'. These are the common examples of *prosopopoeia* in the halls of law today.

Such attribution of agency and thus, potentially, responsibility and liability to objects can be traced, according to the philosopher and literary critic Miguel Tamen, to the origins of ancient Greek law, where a class of Athenian judges presided over a special court in charge of cases brought against inanimate objects.[13] Even English law has a way of dealing with the agency and liability of objects. This was captured in the notion of 'deodand', a legal category in force from the eleventh century. A deodand is an object – a collapsed bridge, a fallen sculpture, a lost cart, a splintered pot – given to God or surrendered to the court to be used or sold to compensate for the death of a human being.[14]

But the object, belonging to men or gods, also had to be investigated. During medieval times the actual practice of forensics was kept alive by people known as 'devil's advocates' – legal experts appointed by the Church to argue against a candidate for canonization by searching for faults or fraud in the account presented as evidence for the miracles the candidate was claimed to have performed. Whereas in other juridical processes of the Church it was the voice of the witness that mattered almost exclusively, hence the emphasis on the combined practices of torture and confession – material forensics, as the science historian

Fernando Vidal shows, was central to the canonization process, and has developed as a model for evidentiary and investigative legal practices using science.[15] Witnesses often reported extraordinary events that they actually believed they had experienced. These miracles were understood as divine interventions in the earthly realm, actions that went beyond the order of divinely created nature. These miracles were mainly healings, sometimes visions, seldom levitations. Their process of ascertainment involved the examination of living bodies and those of the dead, sometimes drops of blood, nails and other carpentry details. Since at least the thirteenth century experts competent in different areas of knowledge – physicians, artists and artisans – were brought in to testify on material objects and be asked whether a natural explanation could be provided. If things had a natural explanation they were not miracles. Forensic science thus developed as a mode of refutation.

Yet it was not until the nineteenth century that the investigation of material evidence took its place next to eyewitness or confessional information, challenging the latter's absolute authority.[16] Forensics started referring almost exclusively to the application of scientific techniques to aid the course of legal process, while the expert witness took the role of the rhetorician and the interpreter. Deodands were finally abolished in England and Wales (Scotland never had deodands) by an Act of Parliament in 1846, mainly in order to protect the railways from lawsuits – when victims could potentially sue for the value of the entire engine – and in 1892, a Russian bell was finally brought back from the Siberian exile to which it was sentenced in 1591.[17]

Science attempted to defetishize forensics, but was not entirely successful. Although, at present, science is becoming the most important arbitrator on matters of legal concern, forensics is not only about scientific inquiry. It also concerns the rhetoric associated with it – the gestures, techniques and technologies of demonstration, methods of theatricality, narrative and dramatization – that can be encompassed by the term 'forensic aesthetics'.[18] It is also about the construction and destruction of the credibility of the experts. In short, it is not only about science as a tool for investigation, but as a means of persuasion and, crucially, as a matter of belief – not that of other scientists in a regulated process of peer review, but of judges, juries or publics that

almost always lack scientific competence.[19] Law and science have
indeed two different methods to ascertain facts and act differently in
relation to probability levels. For scientists, the usual standards of legal
probability, defined as 'beyond reasonable doubt' – the benchmark for
conviction in criminal cases and sufficient to send somebody to the
gallows – or the 'balance of probability' in civil cases, constitute too
low a threshold, and can generally not be accepted in peer review processes as validation of scientific claims. In both domestic and
international law, as Christopher Joyce and Eric Stover dryly remarked
in their book on forensic anthropology, 'lawyers tend to recruit scientists for courtroom appearances much like the way the police shop for
attack-dogs – they look for signs of good breeding coupled with a will-
ingness to take a bite out of an adversary.'[20]

Speaking Bones

Within the framework of human rights and war-crime investigations,
forensic science started to assume its distinctive role from the mid-
1980s and increasingly so after the end of the Cold War. The popular
perception of the wars that erupted in the Balkans and Africa was no
longer predicated on investigations of geopolitical interests and historical process so much as on investigation of the excesses of war
– atrocities, war crimes and breaches of human rights – that were
visited on civilians. War-crime investigations usually call for an analysis
of events more complex than those dealt with by criminal law. War
crimes, like many other wartime events, are produced by a multiplicity
of military agents using a network of different technologies and apparatuses, run by political, institutional and administrative logics. The
forensics of war crime starts with a material remnant to build up a
chain of evidence in reconstructing complex and multi-participant
events, the military networks, and the organization and structures in
which it is embedded. These fields of relation traverse objects rather
than being simply imprinted on them. Ruins and other found objects
must not be regarded in isolation but rather as entry points from which
assembly of connections are traced.

Clyde Snow presents a slide of the skull of Liliana Pereyra, in the 1985 trial of members of the Argentine junta for crimes committed in the 'dirty war' of 1976–1983.

In the context of war-crime investigations, forensic practices emerged in the mid-1980s from within the discipline of forensic anthropology – the application of the science of physical anthropology in legal settings, most often in relation to a victim's remains[21] – and in the crystallization of the newer discipline of forensic archaeology, which applied archaeological principles, techniques and methodologies in the excavating and unearthing of evidence of serious war crimes. Clyde Snow was one of the pioneers of the application of forensic anthropology to state crimes of war. He participated in one of the discipline's founding moments: the exhumation of the remains of Josef Mengele from a wrongly marked grave in the town of Embu, near São Paulo, Brazil, in 1985.[22] Snow later trained the team that conducted the exhumations of the 'disappeared' in Argentina – the first forensic anthropology team working in the context of human rights. Mass graves, starting at this time, turned from sites of commemoration into epistemic resources from which the precise details of war crimes could be reconstructed and entered into the domain of the legal process.

Thomas Keenan explains that 'grave diggers' like Snow were

'flamboyant in their presentation of the logic of what they are doing'.[23] Snow refers to his work as 'osteo-biography', saying that the skeleton contains 'a brief but very useful and informative biography of an individual . . . if you know how to read it'.[24]

By referring to the 'biography' of an object, it becomes clear that it is not only the moment of death but rather the entire process of a life – a sequence of illnesses, incidents and accidents, along with conditions of nutrition, labour and habit – that is fossilized into the morphology and texture of bones, and that a certain blurring of the boundary between object and subject is here undertaken.

In this powerful rhetorical field, the conjunction of bones and ruins makes for a compelling analogy. More recently, forensics has started also acquiring an architectural dimension. With the increasing urbanization of conflict, representations of the built environment are being called as evidence in international courts, tribunals and the media. Geospatial data and high-resolution satellite imagery of destroyed buildings are often used as evidence in court. The presentation of architecture as evidence in court is currently taking place during trials in the International Criminal Tribunal for the former Yugoslavia, where at the beginning of the process, fragments of buildings (and photographs of them) emerged from private homes, gardens and storage sheds, allowing both sides to argue that a different version of events had transpired, using the found and alleged rubble as evidence to substantiate their claims.[25] This process demonstrates that often the evidence precedes, and may call forth, the construction of the forum. The evidence of war crimes in the former Yugoslavia was instrumental in the establishment of the ICTY in 1993. It was the destruction of buildings – religious and civic buildings but also many homes – that became the most visible evidence of ethnic cleansing and genocide. But a destroyed building points to more than the fact of its destruction; it contains information about the means thereof. Ruins are a form of media. They store and, with some help from their 'interpreters', also transmit information about the effects of historical processes. Forensic architecture aspires to transform the built environment from an illustration of alleged violations to a source of knowledge, however incomplete – to enable elucidation from the form and disposition of ruins something of the events that led to a building's destruction. From the perspective of forensics, the ruin has an 'architecture' in which controversial events and political processes are reflected and from which they might be reconstructed and analysed.

Forensic architects must assume that historical events can be reconstructed through structural calculations, blast analysis and a determination of the failure point of structures. In forensic architecture, structural and blast engineers are the interpreters of history. But buildings can provide evidence even when they are in their built form and are not destroyed. Buildings appear static but, as architectural conservationists know, they are in constant movement: they expand and contract with temperature and with the slow degeneration of materials. Concrete, plaster and other exposed surfaces register transformation in humidity, air quality, salination and sometimes also the abrupt or violent events that happen to them, or next to them. In this case buildings must be seen as frieze shots in processes of constant formal transformation – they are diagrams of the social fact itself and of the forces and complex flows that are constantly folded into their form.

With reference to the writing of Walter Benjamin, among others, the artist and theorist Hito Steyerl has beautifully expressed the way in which objects may contain the forces that produced them. It is worth bearing architecture in mind when reading the following:

> Objects are hieroglyphs in whose dark prism social relations lay congealed and in fragments. They are nodes, in which the tensions of a historical moment materialize in a flash of awareness or twist grotesquely into the commodity fetish. In this perspective, a thing is never just an object, but a fossil in which a constellation of forces are petrified. Things are never just inert objects, passive items, or lifeless shucks, but consist of tensions, forces, hidden powers, all being constantly exchanged.[26]

Forensics employs techniques that make objects reveal information by subjecting them to additional force. To be analysed, structures often have to be cut apart, broken or dissolved in acid. The forensics might here be reminiscent of the principles of torture, the art of object-interrogation, the inquisition of things and buildings. This is true even if objects and structures, built or destroyed, do not of course contain all the relations that have produced them – processes and forces do not get mechanically materialized – and are never fully transparent and legible.

The Era of Forensics

Transformation in the methodology of investigating war crimes and human rights violations has meant that forensic science has begun invading some of the cultural grounds previously reserved for the testimonies of human witnesses. When the literary critic Shoshana Felman and the psychoanalyst Dori Laub referred to the last decades of the twentieth century as 'the era of the testimony', and the historian Annette Wieviorka as 'the era of the witness', they wanted to describe the time around the end of the last century when the written, recorded, filmed and exhibited testimony of the Holocaust structured our understanding of the problems of the present.[27] Holocaust, trauma and memory studies have made testimony into a significant force in postmodern culture. Engagement with testimony has left its mark in literature, documentary and the visual arts. Politically, testimony has acquired a visible presence in such varied contexts as truth commissions, human rights theories and humanitarian work.[28]

This function of witness testimony was most strongly identified with anti-totalitarian politics: with the survivor and the dissident, the oppressed and the subaltern, the voice of the individual against the arbitrariness of repressive states. It is hard to think of human rights work outside the frame of testimony. The 'original mission' of human rights organizations was, according to a polemic by Robert Bernstein, the founding director of Human Rights Watch (then called Helsinki Watch and engaged mainly with Soviet bloc dissidents), 'to pry open closed societies, advocate basic freedoms and support dissenters . . . like Andrei Sakharov, Natan Sharansky and those in the Soviet gulag.'[29] Bernstein urged HRW to return to this tradition of anti-totalitarian politics, and strongly opposed investigating Israel's actions in Gaza.

In her investigation of humanitarian testimony, Michal Givoni has noted that one of the characteristics of this testimony is that its ethical function exceeds its epistemic one. Testimony, says Givoni, is significant not only for the knowledge it generates, but as an act of identification and compassion – and therefore it manifests an ethical stand that was adopted by human rights organizations. It is not only tasked with revealing and authenticating claims of historical injustice, but furthermore, the validity of testimony in the context of war crimes stems from the capacity to speak at all in face of the horrors of totalitarianism. Ethical rather than only epistemic, the function of testimony in situations of exposing state crimes is primarily in its delivery.[30] While personal testimony has brought histories of violence and abuse into the public domain, the limits of the frame by which historical accounts foreground individual victims rather than collective action have also become apparent. The psychological framework of trauma and the call for compassion rather than for political action tends to depoliticize historical processes and to portray people as passive and pathetic individual victims, and not as members of a collective with its own political claims.[31]

Dying to Speak

As discussed in chapter one, in the 1990s a series of ad hoc international tribunals was established to try the political and military leaders of the former Yugoslavia (1993) and Rwanda (1994), followed by the permanent international tribunal of the International Criminal Court (1998). The ICRC was invested with the power to imprison violators of war crimes, and to prosecute crimes against humanity and genocide. This 'legalization' of human rights accelerated a shift in the function of testimony from one articulated as a public address needing to withstand cross-examination.[32] The consideration of serious crimes now involved not only the ethical and political responsibility of the belligerents, but the criminal liability of individual perpetrators. This also implied a shift of emphasis from testimony to evidence, from speech to medical data, and sometimes from the accounts of living people to the testimony of forensic anthropologists on behalf of bones and dead bodies. The latter type of statement has become a kind of testimony without witness, a phenomenon that might give another, and rather macabre sense, to the ambition of those believers and promoters of testimony's capacity to 'give a voice to the voiceless'.

The difference between a witness and a piece of evidence is that evidence is presented while a witness is interrogated. However, the legal process already tends to blur this distinction in its demand that the witness approximate objectivity, while the presentation of evidence for cross-examination and interrogation have invested some objects with traits of subjectivity.[33] The person designated with the task of speaking for objects must strip off all layers of subjective interpretation and beliefs, and approximate the position of a neutral conduit for the ascertaining of events, turning, in fact, into something of an object herself.

Potentially, therefore, new ways of using forensic sciences have blurred a previously held distinction between evidence, when the law speaks of objects, and the witness, referring to human testimony. The category of the 'material witness', proposed by Susan Schuppli in relation to her investigation of media artefacts, might be the right means to describe the ground between object and subject.[34] If the material witness is conceptually understood, technically unveiled and legally acknowledged as capable of some kind of 'speech', then it too might be interrogated and cross-examined – and of course, through its interpreter, it might also sometimes lie.

An emergent object-oriented juridical culture is part of a general transformation that has directed attention away from a preoccupation with the subjective and linguistic aspects of trauma and memory, and towards the information saturated in the material world. This shift of emphasis from testimony to forensics has been developed in parallel in a number of related areas and refers to a common epistemological model that has become increasingly influential in the contemporary field of human sciences and law, as well as in popular entertainment. Today's legal and political decisions are based upon DNA samples, 3D scans, nanotechnology, the 'enhanced vision' of electromagnetic microscopes and satellite surveillance, biomedical data and air sampling, and extend from the topography of the sea bed to the remnants of destroyed and bombed-out buildings. If popular entertainment is any indicator of the cultural shift towards forensic fetishism then it is significant that – from *CSI* to the novels of Patricia Cornwell and the former forensics expert Kathy Reichs – the scientist–detective has gradually replaced the psychologist/psychoanalyst–detective popular in TV drama throughout the 1980s and 1990s.[35]

Similarly, until the last decade of the twentieth century, medical diagnosis was still largely undertaken through interviews with patients and an oral 'taking of medical history', while physical examination was tasked mainly with corroborating these symptoms. But with recent advances in imaging and laboratory techniques, the relative weight of oral 'history taking' has decreased. Diagnosis is now an algorithmic process, relying on the use of interactive computer programs that allow physicians to 'experience' a visual representation of what is going on inside the patient's body. This is part of an emphasis on evidence-based medicine designed to assist physicians with decision-making tasks. The 'interviews' that were previously part of the physician's brief – assessing the sociopolitical context of the patient (family, work, stress, beliefs) – have shifted gradually to the responsibility of social workers and psychologists. Perhaps the beginning of the twenty-first century will come to be known as the era of forensics.

Part of what characterizes this 'era of forensics' is a reaction to and perhaps an overcompensation for the indeterminate and fragile voice of the victim – until recently the sign of a traumatized experience that became a potential liability in the intense legal battles taking place in the new international tribunals. Since testimony thus conceived was imbued with so much ethical and cultural significance, the tilt from it towards the interpreted 'material witness' must open up a new and different cultural dimension. But this is not one in which the misanthropic object emerges as a stable and fixed alternative to humane uncertainties, ambiguities and anxieties. Rather, in contemporary forensics, and through the thick field of interpretation and cross-investigation, the problems associated with human testimony – those of the subject – seem to be somewhat reproduced as the problems of the object.

The Forensics of Forensics

Indicative of the forensic shift in war-crime investigation is a development within Human Rights Watch of a practice that the organization calls 'humanitarian battle damage assessment'. The first time HRW undertook this kind of analysis was in 1999, when it investigated the bombing of Belgrade during the Kosovo war. Steve Goose, director of the organization's revealingly termed Arms Division, explained that HRW 'more or less invented the methodology of doing "humanitarian battle damage assessment" . . . the military does its own battle assessment damage, looking at how weapons worked. We do an assessment of how the weapons impacted on civilians. We try to figure out why they were killed.'[36] It was the expansion of HRW's analysis in this new field that led to the hiring of Marc Garlasco.

The distance between the work of human rights organizations and the military was closing. Until the end of the Cold War, all human rights organizations could do was to 'mobilize shame', engage in advocacy and raise awareness. In the late 1990s, the collaboration between human rights organizations and militaries entered a new phase during the 'humanitarian interventions' – actual or proposed – in central Africa and the Balkans. Responding to the inaction and neutrality of the EU, US and UN in the face of ethnic cleansing and genocide in Bosnia and Rwanda, human rights groups were among the most vocal advocates of military intervention. In the 1990s the human rights world had entered into the thick of organized mass violence. During the Clinton administration, Human Rights Watch became one of the most influential pro-intervention lobbies. With close connections to the State Department, it pushed hard for US military action to end the violence in ex-Yugoslavia and Somalia. Under George W. Bush, however, HRW ceded ground to the neoconservatives in its influence on policy. The post-9/11 military interventions in Iraq and Afghanistan no longer needed the encouragement of groups like HRW. Waging war for human rights was more the British than the American justification for the Iraq war, but it played a role in the justification of the war on both sides of the Atlantic, regardless of the fact that the main human rights groups did not advocate for it, and some overtly objected to it.

The relationship between human rights organizations and the military now entered another phase. In order to maintain their relevance and influence, HRW and other groups started to shift their attention from attempts to influence political decision-makers to calls for intervention – they increasingly sought to remain neutral with regard to the causes or justification of wars – and concentrated on the way militaries actually fought them, seeking to influence the conduct of war on the tactical level.[37] The attention thus shifted from the international law frame of *jus ad bellum* (the 'right to wage war') to *jus in bello* (the laws of war) – a legal frame that includes analysis of weapons capabilities and their proportional application, and the legal problems of bombing, counterinsurgency, occupation and military government, as these could be read in the forensics of bodies and ruins.

At the turn of the millennium, military advisers started gaining jobs in many humanitarian and human rights organizations as an institutional register of this new proximity to violence. Former military personnel were greatly in demand by those institutions who saw in their expertise, experience and professional connections a common asset and a bridge to the military. Militaries grew to regard human rights groups not as enemies, but as constructive and enabling critics. Agreeing on the common ground of the necessity to control, reduce and make military violence more efficient, each of these organizations agreed, for its own reasons, about the importance of the 'lesser evil' in reducing civilian casualties.

Garlasco is perhaps the best example of this emerging type of human rights analyst, at a time when human rights practices were themselves in the process of being transformed. Garlasco's hiring and his later work for HRW are part of a larger transformation by which the expression of care for victims was replaced by attempts to uncover the mechanisms of violations as they were reflected in both the objects doing the violation (weapons) and the violated objects (ruins). The cultural transformation that crested with 'the Garlasco affair' was of course bigger than Garlasco. Having had a significant effect on the human rights world, though, it was more than simply another symptom.

Photographs courtesy of HRP 2010.

The images above are taken from the video of a lecture on war crimes in Gaza that Garlasco delivered at Bard College in April 2009. In it, Garlasco discussed the investigation of the destruction of the neighbourhood of Zeitun, south of Gaza City, which was almost entirely obliterated during the 2008–9 invasion.[38] During the Gaza war of 2008–9 Human Rights Watch asked for Israel's permission to enter the strip; but Israel refused. Garlasco and the rest of the HRW team entered through Egypt a few days after the ceasefire was declared. An amateur photographer, Garlasco took the photograph of a woman sitting steadfastly in front of the rubble of her destroyed house. It is an image typical of those taken by human rights researchers when presenting evidence for violations together with their individual victims. But these photos – and their mobilization – encapsulate the shift in emphasis from victims to material forensics. In discussing the image, the elements of the photograph Garlasco points to, the things he chooses to interrogate and narrate, are actually registered in the image's background. Sometimes his silhouette completely obscures that of the woman. At this point in the lecture, he unpacked a set of events by sifting through the chaotic rubble and trash that are the remains of that woman's house. He sees in this rubble a wealth of information: the differences among the tread marks of tanks, armoured personnel carriers and D9 armoured bulldozers. He described the process of his investigation to me:

Gaza, 2009. Photograph by Kai Wiedenhöfer.

When I arrived at Zeitun I saw only four homes untouched. I figured out they must have been the headquarters or the OPs [observation posts] for the soldiers, the anchors of the operation. The rest of the neighbourhood was reduced to all kinds of crushed concrete, iron bars and a lot of rubbish . . . We needed to reconstruct the way this destruction took place . . . From this rubble I wanted to put together the battle story. I looked in the destroyed structures and the surrounding areas for signs of military activity and of exchanges of fire between Israeli and Palestinian forces . . . Aerial bombardment, artillery fire, tank fire and small arms fire have each their specific signature . . .[39]

Garlasco based his interpretation work on a general classification of recurring types of ruins. His description is like that of an archaeologist, investigating a past that has barely passed. Caterpillar D9 Bulldozers create ruins that sometimes look like pyramids or collapsed houses of cards: 'the D9 [armoured bulldozer] takes the corners of the build- ings . . . the central pillars are left standing while the edges of the building collapse and fold outwards.'[40]

Gaza, 2009.
Photograph by Kai Wiedenhöfer.

This type of ruin, now to be seen throughout the Gaza Strip, is the signature of Israeli aggression in the last decade. About one hundred armoured D9 bulldozers were used in Gaza, including some unmanned and remotely controlled ones – together the largest number ever deployed simultaneously – accounting for about half of the 15,000 destroyed or damaged structures. Armoured bulldozers can be deployed under fire, while other forms of destruction must be undertaken in a more controlled fashion by military engineers. The signature of the latter type of destruction is the 'pancake' form of ruin. Garlasco describes how engineers use dynamite or 'anti-tank landmines as demolition explosives . . . and set the charges next to, or in cavities cut within, all internal columns throughout the building. This makes the floor slabs come down on top of each other like a pancake.'

Different types of aerial bombs, of course, produce different types of ruin. When a multi-storey building is bombed from the air, the explosion

occurs on the top floors, often leaving some lower floors standing. Delay-fuse aerial bombs, on the other hand, pierce all floors of the building, burrowing into the foundation before detonating, thereby making the building collapse upon itself with the damage circumscribed to a relatively smaller space.

In his investigation, Garlasco also found signs of a new Israeli strategy: small-scale craters caused by small explosions on what were the roofs of destroyed buildings. These were the results of what Israeli military lawyers called the 'knock on the roof' procedure. In it the Israeli military fires low-explosive 'teaser' bombs or missiles onto houses designated for destruction, with the intention of making an impact strong enough to scare the inhabit-ants into escaping their home before it is destroyed completely with bulldozers or explosives a minute or two later. Upon being hit by this bomb, the residents of such a 'warned house' – if they understand that the impact on their house was indeed 'a message' – have to make a choice: leave the house for a terrifying journey outdoors, or stay and risk being killed. This procedure, according to an officer at the international-law division, embodied the military's humanitarian approach to war – an

Gaza, 2009.
Photograph by Kai Wiedenhöfer.

innovation in the 'technologies of warning'. He explained the logic of such warnings: 'The people who go into a house despite a warning do not have to be taken into account in terms of injury to civilians, because they are voluntary human shields. From the legal point of view, [once warned] I do not have to show consideration for them.' The ability to communicate a warning during a battle is indeed technologically complicated. Battle spaces are messy and confusing environments. This interpretation of international humanitarian law is aimed at shifting people between legal designations, turning 'non-combatants' into voluntary 'human shields' who can thus be killed. To communicate a 'warning' can indeed save a life, but here this principle ended up rendering every house in the strip into a potential 'legitimate' target whose destruction would have been otherwise in contravention of IHL.[41]

Garlasco's reconstruction of events from the rubble left behind was complicated by the presence of ruins dating to different periods. The Gaza Strip was continuously attacked by the Israeli military for more than a decade.

Sometimes different bits of destruction and different piles of rubble could be told apart only by the fact that vegetation was growing in the older ones.

Starting from these general types, Garlasco looked for 'irregularities in the pattern of destruction': secondary explosions, which might designate an ammunition cache; or a fire fight, which registered in bullet holes around windows. These windows sometimes had to be salvaged from under ruins. Identifying a particular incident within the rubble, Garlasco then tried to weave together a series of connections and combine them within a larger narrative.

Back in New York, the HRW team would combine eyewitness interviews, historical and material research to reconstruct the battle story and point out the moments when the excess of violence meant a crime had taken place. This material was then evaluated in relation to the legal categories of 'military necessity', 'distinction,' 'proportionality' and 'weapon choice'. 'After being in Afghanistan, Iraq, Georgia, Burma, I can no longer say if this destruction was wrong or right. I can only say whether it was legal or illegal,' he says. It seems as if legal categories have completely taken the place of political and ethical ones.

Garlasco's analysis of the destruction of Zeitun pointed to war crimes

Gaza, 2009.
Photograph by Kai Wiedenhöfer.

having been committed: 'While bulldozer destruction might have occurred during battle, controlled destruction must have occurred after battle in prepa- ration for the "day after" – usually to "design the battlefield" in a way that would favour future operations. This is a war crime of wanton destruction not necessitated by the war.' Most destruction has indeed taken place in order to shape the battle space for a future engagement. Homes along main roads, or along the Gaza perimeter fence, were destroyed to allow safer movement for military vehicles along them. It was a textbook case of design by destruction – the shaping of the battle space to suit operational needs.

The hiring of Garlasco by Human Rights Watch not only marked the shift, previously discussed, from the human witness to the material object, but from a focus on the victims of war to an analysis of the mechanisms

Gaza, 2009.
Photograph by Kai Wiedenhöfer.

of the violation of law. This testifies to a wider assumption, now held by most human rights groups: that a detailed knowledge of technological development and military capability, combined with an understanding of the military systems that employ and weave these technologies together, is crucial to their work; that violations exist in the conjunction of technologies, operational procedures and political motivations.

One of the best examples is HRW's report on civilian deaths as a result of drone attacks in Gaza, 'Precisely Wrong', prepared by Garlasco and published in June 2009. It is an astounding foray into the technical capabilities of these weapons that reads sometimes like an advertisement in a military journal. It has also left some of Garlasco's colleagues and board members in HRW feeling uncomfortable. Here is a quote from it:

The drone-launched missiles detonate above the ground, which creates a narrow, relatively shallow crater from missile parts not involved in fragmentation hitting the ground. The detonation of the warhead inside the fragmentation sleeve creates an expanding sphere of fragments that fly out. The fragments are composed of tungsten, a dense inert metal, and their heavy weight and small size (3 mm cubes) create a rapid drop-off in kinetic energy that keeps the area of effect relatively small – approximately 20 metres in diameter.[42]

The report goes on to connect this technology to questions of new responsibilities and liabilities.

Considering these are the new terms by which human rights organizations operate, Garlasco should be acknowledged as one of the most efficient human rights analysts in recent years, as well as a key figure in the development of forensic architecture. Colin Kahl, a professor of security studies at Georgetown University, was quoted by the *Washington Post* as saying that Garlasco 'knows more about airstrikes than anyone in the world who isn't in the military currently.'[43] Indeed, in the years leading up to the Gaza investigation, he became something of a celebrity within the field of conflict analysis, prominently interviewed on news channels, and in newspapers and documentary films worldwide.[44] He has also been an extremely effective advocate for placing military violence under check. His work as HRW investigator on cluster bombs employed in the American invasion of Iraq in 2003, in Lebanon during Israel's 2006 attack, and by the Russian army during the Georgia war of 2008, was central to the UN's ratification of the Convention on Cluster Munitions, which eventually banned these weapons. His investigation of torture in Abu Ghraib helped Senator John McCain pass his anti-torture amendment in 2005.[45]

Forensic Fetishism

The controversy that unfolded around Marc Garlasco in September 2009 involved the most extreme manifestation of the contemporary burgeoning appetite for forensics and our present obsession with object analysis and science. In the process of campaigning against Richard Goldstone

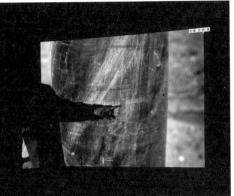

Photographs courtesy of HRP, 2010.

and HRW's investigation into the 2008–9 Gaza invasion, NGO Monitor, an organization with links to Israel's ministry of foreign affairs, seized on the discovery of Garlasco's interest in Nazi memorabilia. It ran a story whose headline included the phrase: 'Marc Garlasco's Nazi Fetish!'[46] To the people that knew him, the implication that Garlasco had an anti-military or anti-Israeli bias was ironic: among HRW personnel he was considered to be one of the closest to the US military and to the Israeli military, the one who could – and did – speak their professional language.

Human Rights Watch's reaction was indecisive. Initially, it defended Garlasco. But a few days later, following prominent coverage of the affair in the *New York Times*, and presumably under pressure from HRW's donors, it decided to suspend him on full pay while commissioning an external firm to produce an independent report which, by mutual agreement, has not been made public to this day. In February 2010, following this investigation, Garlasco resigned. A year later he found work to suit his skills with the UN in Afghanistan.

In a posting written in the wake of the controversy, Garlasco sought to defend his reputation, explaining that he is 'a military geek' who collects 'the weapons that I study and the shrapnel I analyze.'[47] The fascination with militaria that his detractors called 'fetishism' involved, he suggested, the very same qualities that drove him to become a forensic analyst, and to be good at his work.[48] Garlasco's response to his detractors must thus be taken

Marc Garlasco examining munitions. Photograph courtesy of Marc Garasco.

seriously. If fetishism can be defined as the attribution of an inherent power and a certain agency to inanimate objects or technologies, then forensics must be understood as one of the most distinct contemporary manifestations of fetishism. A degree of fetishism is certainly implicit in any attribution to the object of the agency of a witness.

Here the fetish is not the mystifying and obfuscating vale which masks the true way that objects are made in the world – a feature of capitalism that Marx identified in commodity fetishism. In our story, the fetish marks a certain attraction to the objects of violence and the intensity of delving into their investigation – forensic fetishism as the return to the object, to the non-human in human rights work. This conjunction of forensics and fetish is also a rather astoundingly comical demonstration of what Bruno Latour called the 'factish', a term he coined to merge the objectivity of facts with the mysterious attraction and autonomous power of fetishes. Objects, Latour explains, must be regarded as existing between the scientific and the totemic, 'a combination of facts and fetishes that makes it obvious that the two have a common element of fabrication.'[49] Forensic fetishism might thus differ from the commodity or the sexual fetish, in the sense of the latter being objects imbued with affect and desire, and be rather understood as an object holding in itself a diagram of relations – 'hieroglyphs in whose dark prism social relations lie congealed and in fragments . . . fossils in which a constellation of forces are petrified.'[50] Methodological fetishism is the condition of a microphysical analysis in which the part or detail becomes an entry point from which the

Marc Garlasco examining unexploded ordnance, Gaza 2009. Photograph courtesy of Marc Garlasco.

reconstruction of larger processes, events and social relations, conjunctions of actors and practices, structures and technologies, may take place.

The Thirtieth Civilian

When I heard about Garlasco's suspension from HRW I asked to meet him. Garlasco was still shaken by events. I offered to help, in pointing out that I believed that his forensics work was credible not in spite of his controversial collection – the so-called fetish – but rather, significantly, because of it. Although Garlasco didn't feel it was the best line of defence, we went on talking. When I mentioned that HRW surely must have known about his hobby, Garlasco answered: 'When hiring me in 2003 HRW knew of much worse: that I had been involved in the killing of about 250 civilians in Iraq.'

Indeed, as has since been since reported, before joining HRW as military analyst, Garlasco worked for seven years as an intelligence analyst in the US Defense Intelligence Agency at the Pentagon. His job was to undertake target selection and planning for aerial bombing in both the 1998 air attack on Iraq and the NATO attack on Serbia the following year. Garlasco was also in the Pentagon on the morning of 9/11 when American Airlines Flight 77 hit the building. In the months leading up to the US invasion of Iraq in February 2003 he became 'chief of high-value

Computer simulation of a blast sequence. Image courtesy of Hinman Consulting Engineers, 2005.

targeting'. In this context, 'high value' meant the killing of political leaders in 'targeted assassinations', tracking and designing the aerial attacks that were intended to kill Saddam Hussein and other Ba'ath leaders in the first hours of the invasion.

A central part of planning these missions involved a calculus otherwise known as 'collateral damage estimate'. This helped, under the principle of proportionality, to establish the 'correct balance of civilian casualties in relation to the military value of a mission'. For every single attack on a political or military leader – and these attacks were mostly on civilian apartment buildings where the suspecting 'targets' felt camouflaged or protected by being close to civilians – Garlasco had to undertake an analysis that would estimate the number of civilians who would be killed. The projection was based on specialized software first introduced during the air campaign over Serbia and originally called 'Bug Splat'; later – when the connotation of civilian death with disinfection was seen as 'politically unhelpful' – it was renamed 'fast collateral damage', or Fast CD.[51] The software included algorithms resembling those employed in architecture, structural engineering and urban planning. It synthesized environmental factors such as the size of a building, its construction materials and techniques, the amount of steel in the structure and glass in its envelope, and the population density within and around it (which varied at different times of day). All these were calculated against other factors: the size and

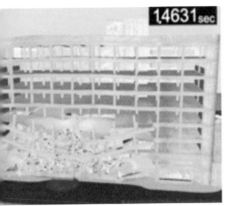

type of bomb, its fuse and the direction of the attack. In general, the software was used to estimate the number of civilian casualties in relation to the interaction between types of buildings and different munitions. Pentagon briefers thought of this as a 'mitigation technique' – a means of reducing the damage and devastation of war – and explained that international law can be complied with through a correct use of the appropriate algorithm, and a proportionate number of civilian deaths.

A detailed analysis of the sequence of collapse caused by bomb damage, for example, can be undertaken to very high precision at present. An expert in the forensic analysis of buildings described in technical detail how structural engineering might be combined with blast engineering to produce a milisecond-by-milisecond account of death and destruction. I reproduce it here because it allows a glimpse into the detail with which blast calculations can be made in relation to structures, and how this can later be applied in projecting and predicting the numbers of casualties.

An explosion is a chemical reaction that causes an extremely rapid release of energy in several forms: sound, heat and shock waves, consisting of highly compressed particles of air propagating radially outward from the explosive source at supersonic velocities. Released energy pushes the air particles out. The shock wave travels across and through the building, and in the process pressure is applied on all the surfaces it encounters. It flows both upward and downward and acts on the floor slabs of the building. The exterior walls bend inward and break, initiating a 'progressive collapse'. Air, as wind, rushes in to fill the vacuum, carrying high-velocity debris and flying bits of glass, causing lacerations; lungs collapse, and eardrums rupture. But most people die within buildings when they collapse upon them.'[52]

In order to work out and verify the prediction of civilian deaths, Garlasco had to familiarize himself with architecture, structural engineering and also with urbanism to understand the variable occupancy of buildings throughout the day:

> It all boils down to energy transfer, which dictates the angle of attack, the time, the fuse . . . how blast energy interacts with the logic of structures. Is it made of wood? Steel is stronger than metal-reinforced concrete. How much glass in the face of the building? What is the soil type in which the foundations are planted? . . . These are calculated against human factors like the number of people within buildings, et cetera.

Material calculations of the extent to which a building will be destroyed are then translated into an expected casualty level.

The magic number in designing the attacks in Iraq, Garlasco recalled, was thirty. 'If the computer came up with thirty anticipated civilians killed, the air-strike had to go to Rumsfeld or Bush personally to sign off. Anything less than thirty could simply go ahead.'[53] In this system of calculation, twenty-nine deaths designates a threshold. Above it, in the eyes of the US military lawyers, is potentially 'unlawful killing'; below it, 'necessary sacrifice'. Although the number was most likely chosen for reasons of its potential resonance in the media, it was argued as an issue of proportionality. For the civilians it marked a potential threshold between life and death.[54]

According to the principle of proportionality, then, targeting resembles a mathematical minimum problem. The abstract and fuzzy ethics of the lesser evil is here translated into objective choices. 'The minimum-size bomb to generate the required effect, the type of explosives within it, the angle of attack, the time of day. In January 2003 when the target packages were "finalized", we had about three hundred targets that were considered "high CD", or high collateral damage, meaning over thirty [anticipated civilians killed] . . . We had the Air Force play with the bomb angles, fusing, bomb tonnage, et cetera, and got that number down to about twenty-five', he explains like a modern-day Pangloss. 'I don't think people really appreciate the gymnastics that the US military goes through in order to make sure that they're not killing [too many] civilians'.[55]

The Design of Ruins

According to the logic of Garlasco's targeting in Iraq, given that a precise threshold number of 'acceptable' civilian casualties had been imposed on each bombing attack, the principle of 'proportionality' acquired an architectural manifestation. Without a designated limit to the number of civilian casualties, the bombers would simply have dropped a large-enough bomb to make sure that the entire building and its surroundings were flattened. The need to keep to the given threshold of civilian deaths, however, necessitated the targeted destruction of building parts – a surgical form of destruction which might involve the destruction of top floors within a tower block, or of single wings in a sprawling building where the target is thought to be hiding and when no more than twenty-nine people would be killed. 'Material proportionality' in this context should therefore be understood as the effect of proportionality analysis. The practice of the design of ruins combines the calculation of life and death with those of structural stability.

The Iraq war started on 20 March 2003 with an attempted aerial assassination of Saddam Hussein, which failed but killed fifteen civilians. On 5 April, the bombing of the supposed safe house of Ali Hassan al-Majid, known as 'Chemical Ali', in the port city of Basra, was carried out according to Garlasco's planning. Seventeen civilians were killed; al-Majid, though, was elsewhere. On 7 April another attacks, targeting Saddam Hussein in the al-Mansur district of Baghdad, killed eighteen civilians. On 9 April, Baghdad fell. Each of the fifty targeted assassination strikes undertaken in the early stages of the war failed to kill the person they were meant for, yet each killed close to the 'permitted' and 'proportional' number of civilians. Although he did not agree with the rationale behind the Iraq war, Garlasco continued to work for the Pentagon:

'Whether you agree with the aim of war or not, it is going to happen. I stayed on because I wanted to do it in the best way I could. I had responsibility to the pilots and the civilians.' That he understood his responsibility towards civilians (to upwards of the twenty-ninth civilian one must add) demonstrates the logic of this new form of proportional violence: a violence that both kills and saves, a violence that calculates and determines the threshold between life and death. 'I didn't try to kill civilians . . . I focused on military targets and tried my very best every day *to minimize* civilian casualties'. This is a startling testimony for the way the economy of violence structures the humanitarian present.

The Devil's Advocate

After the fall of Baghdad, Garlasco, feeling uncomfortable with the war, the way it was developing and his role within it, resigned from the Pentagon. He then answered a job advert for Human Rights Watch, got an interview, and got the job. HRW gave him a several-weeks-long course in human rights before dispatching him to Iraq. His first task for HRW included, remarkably, a review of the results of his previous job: to study the impact of the aerial bombardment and to contribute to the writing of a report on the aerial war in whose planning he had participated while in the Pentagon.[56] His first report included, thus, reviews of his own previous actions. He knew of course where to look for the ruins – he had participated in drawing the target bank. Now he stood at the 'scene of the crime', which he had previously studied only on screens; it was his first time in Iraq, in front of the ruins he had helped create.[57] The resulting report, entitled 'Off Target', was generally critical of the aerial war. It found that attacks which targeted the Iraqi leadership had resulted in the largest number of civilian deaths of the bombing campaign. It did, however, note that the proportionality analysis undertaken by the Pentagon had been effective in reducing the number of civilian casualties.[58] As outrageous as the calculus of civilian death appears, the limit of twenty-nine civilians, like any other number that was or could have been used – indeed, the fact that there was a limit at all – was a form of mitigation based on the introduction of IHL principles into military planning. It is the calculation and measuring of the collateral that made the bombing potentially comply with IHL.

Garlasco's trip to Iraq is important because it marks the moment when techniques and technologies used to 'design the ruins' were employed in the diagnosis of the actual damage inflicted. The moment when Garlasco stood in front of and looked at the ruins could be interpreted as the hinge around which the making of ruins turns into the reading of ruins. Garlasco told me that this moment – standing in the centre of Baghdad and in Basra before the ruins that he himself had caused – 'made me shiver'.

The trajectory of technological development that culminates in forensic architecture can be summed up in the following sequence. Developments in precision bombing brought about the possibility of aerial targeted assassination. Developments in these techniques also enabled the prediction of material damage, and the number of civilian deaths. These in turn allowed for proportionality analysis to be articulated around precise numbers. Finally, now in different hands, they have also enabled ruins to be studied and interpreted as to the details of the attack. It is in this context of technological continuum, and its political and tactical implementation, that the practice of 'forensic architecture' relies on the very technologies of bombing whose results it aims to monitor and reconstruct.

'My forensics is a reverse engineering of the process of military destruction,' Garlasco told me. 'When studying a ruin, the first thing I do is to think how I would have planned the attack.'[59] His former career at the Pentagon and the targeted bombings for which he was responsible were public knowledge. Indeed, they were the subject of considerable media interest: Garlasco's military past and strategic know-how were the very things that gave him the visibility and credibility he enjoyed as a human rights analyst, while it gave HRW the authority it needed in making its 'humanitarian battle damage assessments'. To put it another way, a public that was so shocked about the revelations over Garlasco's collection of Nazi-era paraphernalia saw nothing strange about a man who had presided over several attacks that killed civilians working for a human rights organization. In 2008, the *Washington Post* painted a glowing portrait of Garlasco, 'the man on both sides of the air war debate',[60] while elsewhere, he was often asked about 'crossing the lines'.

Yet the idea that Garlasco has crossed any lines, in any significant sense, is misleading. While his move from the Pentagon to Human Rights Watch was widely depicted as a kind of redemption story – like the saint whose virtues could only ever be as great as his previous sins – such a reading misses the extent to which human rights groups and militaries have become intertwined in their methods and aims, and the process by which, in 'forensic architecture', destruction and diagnostics have become interchangeable. As the forensics of past atrocities takes such prominent place in present political analysis, another narrative model must be considered. This one belongs to the detective fiction genre: the reading of history from the structures it violates is not a benign process of tuning in or learning to listen; it offers no redemption; rather, it belongs to the same order of violence that it comes to investigate. Today's forensic investigators of violence move alongside its perpetrators, morphing into them just as the detective becomes one with the criminal.

Gaza, 2009. Photograph by Kai Wiedenhöfer. The spray paint reads 'Khalil Attar's House' and includes his mobile number.

Epilogue:
The Destruction of Destruction

In the spring of 2009 following the Israeli winter attack, the Gaza-based and Hamas-run Ministry of Public Works and Housing started compiling an archive titled 'A Verification of Building-Destruction Resulting from Attacks by the Israeli Occupation'. This 'book of destruction' – as the archive was soon to be known – contained thousands of entries, each documenting a single building that was completely or partially destroyed, from cracked walls in houses that still stand, to those completely reduced to piles of rubble.[1] In reconstructing the course of events from the investigation of the trash and rubble left behind, this archive is another instance of forensic architecture. Both practical and political, its forensics is however outside the frame of international law.

A year later, in the spring of 2010, I had the opportunity to examine a few hundred of the entries. Each entry included a single, frontal-view photograph of a destroyed building. Each photograph displayed a catalogue number spray-painted onto the walls or onto the rubble itself. Sometimes, the building had been so badly pulverized that there was no longer any clear surface left to spray-paint the code on. Instead, the numbers had been jotted down on pieces of paper, cards or sheets of plastic and placed among the rubble or held up in front of the camera at the moment the photograph was taken (N3004-101).

Catalogue entries such as G10177-01, N30049-3, K1086-01, R1002-03 designate the location of each building. 'G' stands for Gaza City, 'N' for the northern sector of the Strip, 'K' for Khan Younis and 'R' for Rafah.

The digits following the letters designate the relevant neighbourhood, road and plot. The classification is based on an area grid system that covers the entire Gaza Strip. Each existing and potential building site in Gaza – those ruined and those still intact – have thus been designated as a possible site of destruction. Each entry in the 'book of destruction' contained several other documents, detailing the size of the plot and the building, the type of construction – most commonly cast concrete frames with unrendered cinderblocks – and, when the municipality could get hold of them, plans of the buildings in question. Unable to avoid the temptation of exercising their authority even over the ruins, sometimes the ministry employees undertaking the survey noted that a destroyed building or an extension had been built without planning permission.

Significantly, each file also recorded how the damage to the building was inflicted. There were boxes to be ticked next to several pre-designated categories: 'destroyed by armoured D9 bulldozers', 'bombed from the air' (N2003-02, K6002-11); 'shelled from the ground' (N4005-02, R1002-03); 'directly targeted', 'indirectly struck' or 'controlled demolition by explosives'. Other checked boxes described the state of the building: 'reduced to rubble', 'partially destroyed' or 'still standing but dangerous and requiring demolition'. The archive also includes information about the use of the building – most often residential, sometimes of mixed use with a small shop or a workshop – and the names of the people that owned or lived in it. Each entry included the identity cards and telephone numbers of some of the building's occupants. Many entries included photocopies of UNRWA (UN Relief and Work Association) cards, indicating that the buildings' inhabitants were refugees supported by international welfare. Indeed, the destroyed buildings were mostly home to refugees who lived in the camps of Gaza or in the poor neighbourhoods that ring its cities. In Gaza, where 70 per cent of the population are refugees, the boundaries between camps and neighbourhoods are porous.

The archive tries to clear up the chaos and confusion of the after-attack by organizing the rubble into clear categories. But the reading of these images overspills the classifications under which they were filed. In her reading of photographs of violence and destruction, Ariella Azoulay commented upon the way in which details, accidentally recorded in photographs, could challenge the classification logic intended by the archive makers.[2] Indeed, the 'book of destruction' offers glimpses onto daily realities in Gaza, and the consequences of its domination by Israel. Some photographs show families inhabiting a house still destroyed: having nowhere else to go, they have sealed the gaps between the broken slabs with blankets and nylon sheets, living in and among ruins (N3004-94). Some photographs show people posing in front of the ruins that were their homes (N4022-050, N3004-111). Are they attempting to mark their ownership, their subsequent dispossession and physical survival beyond the life of the building they lived in? Some other photographs show a small gathering of people around sites of destruction (G1014-07). Azoulay also explained that ruins often generate *ad hoc* public spaces – around which people assemble.[3] The visible ruin plays a major role in the public display of the facts of domination and violence; it demonstrates the presence of colonial power even when the colonizer is nowhere to be seen. Before Israel left Gaza in 2005, it demonstrated its control over the enclave by the displays of power that are its settlements. In 1980, as minister in charge of settlements, Ariel Sharon made sure his order was understood when he said he wanted 'the Arabs to see Jewish lights every night 500 metres from them.'[4] After the Israeli military relocated to the Strip's perimeter and destroyed the settlements, inaugurating an era of colonialism without colonies, the destroyed buildings in Gaza – standing like monuments, unrepaired, unrepairable – became the most significant means for the visual affirmation of its domination.

The draft for the future 'book of destruction' has been presented as the Israeli military's 'book of targets in Gaza.' It is a thick blue folder which was passed at the start of 2011 from the outgoing chief of staff, Gabi Ashkenazi, who presided over the destruction of 2008–9, to his successor in a grotesque ceremony. 'There is something symbolic in the transition today of all days,' said the outgoing military chief, 'which is why I want to hand over something I carry with me all the time: the updated book of targets'.[5] This book also contains a biography of certain buildings in the enclave: information about their structure and construction, who lives in them, what they are used for, what should be done to them and how.

*   *   *

The logic of the 'book of destruction', according to its makers – Dr Ibrahim Radwan, the Minister for Public Works, and his director of urban planning, Mohammed al-Ostaz – is that of a property-damage survey, a practical way to account for the necessary work of reconstruction and its cost. But the archive testifies, rather, to a different reality: the impossibility of undertaking any major programme of rebuilding. The entries on the survey are from April and May 2009, three to four months after the destruction took place, but many of the ruins are left unrepaired still. Two years prior to the attack, the importing of cement and other vital construction materials into Gaza had been banned. These materials were classified by Israel as 'dual-use construction materials' suspected of being used equally to build bunkers and reinforce tunnels. Without these materials, the Palestinian ministry could not oversee much more than the documentation of the destruction inflicted by Israel's invasion. This it did thoroughly.

Reporting from Gaza in Spring 2009, Peter Beaumont of the *Guardian* was the first journalist to come across the strange catalogue numbers etched onto the ruins 'fetishistically in blue and green' and traced them back to the ministry. 'Like exhibits in a museum, every house, school and hospital that has been turned into rubble is noted in this book of destruction'.[6] Charges of 'fetishism' seem to haunt the practice of forensics. This is perhaps because forensics is tuned to the 'object quality' of history and its different modes of reification, and because it deals with the protocols and technologies by which objects speak. By invoking the term, Beaumont might have meant to underline the way in which the focus on structures and ruins might mask the story of the war's human casualties. His empathy, responding to a similar instinct of many in the human rights world, is understandable. He went on to find some of the people affected and to retell their stories. But shattered concrete and cinderblocks can reveal something different from the human testimony he gathered. In its impersonal bureaucratic logic, with its surveyors' maps, diagrams, photographs, and captions, and the patterns, repetitions and differences in destruction they reveal, the archive helps capture the relentless magnitude of Gaza's destruction in a different way.

The description and quantification of these crushed buildings functions similarly to the statistics that open W. G. Sebald's *The Natural History of Destruction*, on the Allied destruction of German cities in 1945: '31.1 cubic metres of rubble for every person in Cologne and 42.8 cubic metres for every inhabitant of Dresden';[7] they are the grounds for a historical, political and cultural interrogation of the bombing.

Likewise, writing about the 1755 earthquake in Lisbon, Sharon Sliwinski noted the power of detailed representations of destroyed buildings to generate political identification across borders. The series of copper engravings of the ruined city, produced by the French artist Jacques-Philippe Le Bas in a patient and careful survey undertaken in 1757, circulated widely throughout Europe and the Americas. They were part of what constituted 'the first modern mass media events in which subjects throughout Europe became spectators to a distant catastrophe . . . helping inaugurate a secular notion of human suffering as well as thoughts about its prevention.' It seems as if the universal notion of the 'human' – as much as the question of political rights – could be as effectively captured in the representation of 'non-human things'.[8]

In Palestine, in his poem 'The House Murdered', Mahmoud Darwish also pointed to the house as the most potent object-witness to Palestinian history. In it the crushed glass, iron and cement 'all scatter in fragments like beings': they are the prism through which both private life and common history can be interrogated. 'The house murdered is also mass murder, even if vacant of its residents. It is a mass grave for the basic elements needed to construct a building for meaning.' In the aftermath of destruction, says Darwish, objects yield up their stories. He also provides a list of secondary witnesses:

> stone, wood, glass, iron, cement . . . cotton, silk, linen, papers, books . . . plates, spoons, toys, records, faucets, pipes, door handles, fridges, washing machines, flower vases, jars of olives and pickles, tinned food . . . salt, sugar, spices, boxes of matches, pills, contraceptives, antidepressants, strings of garlic, onions, tomatoes, dried okra, rice and lentils . . . rent agreements, marriage documents, birth certificates, water and electricity bills, identity cards, passports, love letters . . . photographs, toothbrushes, combs, cosmetics, shoes, underwear, sheets, towels . . . Our things die like us, but they don't get buried with us!'[9]

Gazans have been living in and among ruins since at least the early twentieth century. Accounts of rubble in Gaza, generated from the destruction visited during the battle fought between the British Egyptian Expeditionary Force under the command of General Allenby and the Ottoman army in March 1917, can be found in diaries and correspondence of British officials such as Charles Robert Ashbee of the Arts and Crafts movement in the 1920s, and in those of British District Commissioners until as late as 1938.[10] The wars of 1947–9, the military incursions of the 1950s, the 1956 war, the 1967 war, the 1972 'counter-insurgency' in the refugee camps of Gaza, the first intifada of 1987–91, and the waves of destruction brought about during the second intifada of the 2000s, have each piled new layers of rubble on top of those produced by their predecessors. It is sometimes hard to tell them apart.

When a building, however poor and simple, is destroyed, its representational value is no longer in its façade, but rather in its broken structure now revealed. The 'book of destruction' can also be read as an archive of materials and construction techniques, which themselves reveal something of the history and economy of the area. The images in the archive reveal the fast and rudimentary building technique typical of refugee homes; the relatively low quantity of cement in mortar composition. Refugee homes are structural frames, temporary in as much as they are never completed – they are never-ending construction sites. Their fragile structural skeletons easily succumbed to the steel and explosive hauled at them.

For Israel, refugee homes represent more than piles of materials and human waste to be ploughed through. While the Arab states, and even possibly a Palestinian one, might be accepted as fierce but conventional enemies, only the refugees have a moral and historical claim against the Israeli state that was established in 1948 on the ruins of their society. The war on refugees is an ongoing form of violence that seeks not only to destroy refugee life and property but also to restructure 'refugeeness' – that feature of Palestinian political identity. This kind of war is undertaken both by destruction and reconstruction – and attempts to make the refugee problem disappear by architectural means. Israeli military destruction in refugee camps is often followed by attempts at development, programmes for 'proper housing' and urbanization.

In 2010, the same power that destroyed Gaza sought to supervise its reconstruction. In the wake of its assault on the international flotilla that set out to deliver supplies to Gaza, Israel eased the siege, allowing in some construction materials. The Israeli military's 'humanitarian coordination office' informed international agencies that they needed to obtain its approval for every construction project, however. The power of Israel to affect the reconstruction is exercised by regulating the entry of steel, gravel and cement through the terminals in the Gaza perimeter fence.[11] It gave approval mainly for internationally funded projects – also approved by the Palestinian Authority in Ramallah, the Hamas government's political opponents.

For refugees, camps were shelters for the reconstruction of personal and social life, but were also seen as sites of great political significance, the material testimony of what was destroyed and 'all that remains' of more than four hundred cities, towns and villages forcefully cleansed throughout Palestine in the Nakba of 1947–9.[12] This is the reason that refugees sometimes refer to the destruction of camps as 'the destruction of destruction'. The camp is not a home, it is a temporary arrangement, and its destruction is but the last iteration in an ongoing process of destruction.[13] This rhetoric of double negation – the negation of negation – tallies well with what Saree Makdisi, talking about the Israeli refusal to acknowledge the Nakba, has termed 'the denial of denial,' which is, he says, 'a form of foreclosure that produces the inability – the absolutely honest, sincere incapacity – to acknowledge that a denial and erasure have taken place because that denial and erasure have themselves been erased in turn and purged from consciousness.'[14] What has been denied is continuously repeated: Israel keeps on inflicting destruction on refugees and keeps on denying that a wrong has been done – as testified by its denial of the findings of international reports on the Gaza war and its inability to accept responsibility for the destruction it causes. The destroyed village of 1948 and the destroyed camp of 2009 stand thus on a historical continuum of ongoing destruction and denial. The 'book of destruction' documents the ongoing Nakba; it is a 'single catastrophe, which unceasingly piles rubble on top of rubble . . .'

What form of practice is called upon by the 'destruction of destruction'? Does it designate salvation and the beginning of return? Or is it simply a call for the removal of the dust and rubble, for cleaning up and starting all over again?

With camps understood as the destruction of that which was already destroyed, forensics – the hermeneutics of this rubble – is faced with a more complex, double-edged challenge. It is not simply tasked with uncovering past events and the way destruction has occurred, but with the means of evaluating future works. This forensics must look simultaneously forwards and backwards: connecting the destruction of the present – the rubble piling before our feet – to a longer and ongoing history of destruction and displacement thus far denied; and also, pragmatically and practically, with evaluating the necessary works needed for reconstruction and their cost. Both these perspectives are eminently political; they are different from each other, but their power is in being practiced simultaneously.[15]

The predominant conceptual frame by which refugee camps are understood is one in which every physical improvement at present is a potential threat to the provisional nature of the camp. Urbanizing the camp, making it permanent, might sacrifice the 'right of return' to which its temporariness otherwise testifies. But a new generation of Palestinian scholars and architects – Ismael Sheikh Hassan and Sari Hanafi in Lebanon, and Nasser Abourahme and Sandi Hillal in Palestine prominent among them – have attempted to challenge the conceptualization of refugee habitats as mere repositories of national memory.[16] The stronger the camp, they argue, the better the chances of it becoming a political space, a platform on which refugees' political claims could be articulated and the struggle continued. In Nahr el Bared in Lebanon after its destruction by the Lebanese army in 2007, and in the camps of Gaza and those of the West Bank that shouldered much of the burden of ongoing resistance and paid its price, they worked with refugee communities and UN agencies to pick up the rubble, to design and promote programmes for camp improvement and upgrading – but not just any programmes or any plans. The plans they struggled for resisted all attempts to remove refugees from the area of the camp and to dispere them in new neighbourhoods. For those that remained in the camp, and for those that live just outside it, they sought to reinforce the camp as a vibrant living space with community services and political institutions. An improved camp with open access, public spaces, functioning institutions, updated physical and communication infrastructure and better homes, is not a negation of the right of return but rather an instrument for its reinforcement. Such a camp could provide a platform for political mobilization. This point of view rejects both the accommodation to an unjust political reality and the *politique du pire* that seeks to maintain misery and invest it with political meaning. The reconstruction of Gaza, when and if made possible, might mean the arrival of some international organizations and state donors with a multiplicity of agendas and the means to pursue them. Facing this well-meaning aid, refugees will have to adopt a delicate process of navigating between poles. Homes must be rebuilt, infrastructure laid out, camps and life improved, not instead of but rather in order to support political rights and the continuous struggle to achieve them. This will surely still be much less than perfect but it is certainly not the choice of the lesser evil.

Palestinian National Authority
Ministry of Public Works & Housing

السلطة الوطنية الفلسطينية
وزارة الأشغال العامة والإسكان

استمارة تدقيق أضرار هدم كلي لمبنى سكني نتيجة اعتداءات الاحتلال الإسرائيلي

رقم المنطقة	رقم المبنى
N 40 05	02

صفحة ....1... من ..6..

القسم (1) معلومات العنوان وسبب الهدم

7.1 تاريخ المعاينة	6.1 تاريخ الضرر	5.1 الرقم التنظيمي	4.1 الشارع	3.1 الحي	2.1 البلدية	1.1 المحافظة
2009 / 4 / 16	2008 / 12 / 29	44	شارع فرعي	رباط	بيت لحم	الشمال

		14.1 حدود المبنى	13.1 الأرض	12.1 مساحة الأرض(م2)	11.1 القطعة	10.1 رقم الحوض	9.1 رقم القطعة	8.1 بالقرب من :
الشمال: سبع الغزي 12								
الجنوب: حارة ميرعة			☐ ملك ☐ حكومة ☐ أوقاف	400	4/A	18	1766	
الشرق: محمد يونس 4/8								
الغرب:								

15.1 سبب الهدم الكلي	☑ قصف مباشر	☐ قصف مجاور لـ	☐ تفجير	☐ تجريف
16.1 حالة المبنى عند المعاينة	☑ قائم ويحتاج إزالة بالكامل	☐ قائم ويحتاج إزالة جزء منه	☐ يشكل خطر على المواطنين	☐ ركام ☐ أخرى

القسم (2) معلومات عن المبنى

3.2 رقم الجوال /أقرب رقم	2.2 رقم الهوية / جواز السفر	1.2 اسم المبنى أو المالك(رباعي)
0 9 7 3 6 2 8 5	9 0 5 8 1 2 4 8 3	عيسى محمد سالم ابو حلته

4.2 رقم الهاتف /أقرب رقم	5.2 نوع المبنى رقم :	☐ فيلا ☐ دار ☑ عمارة ☐ براكية ☐ خيمة

6.2 مساحة سطح البناء (م2)	162	7.2 عدد الطوابق	5	8.2 نوع سطح المبنى	☐ قرميد ☑ باطون 162	☐ اسبست ☐ صاج ☐ أخرى

9.2 استخدام المبنى	☑ للسكن ☐ للعمل ☐ للعمل والسكن ☐ أخرى	10.2 عدد الوحدات السكنية	5	عدد الوحدات المشغولة	5	عدد الوحدات الخالية	0

11.2 ملحقات المبنى	☐ سور طوله 20م ارتفاعه(م.ط)	☐ مخزن م2	☐ كراج م2	☐ حديقة م2	☐ أخرى م2

12.2 هل يوجد بدروم ؟	☐ نعم ☑ لا	13.2 مساحة البدروم (م2)	/	14.2 استخدام البدروم	☐ للسكن ☐ للعمل ☐ للسكن والعمل ☐ أخرى

15.2 تشطيب البدروم	☐ فاخر ☐ غير مشطب ☐ متوسط ☐ تحت المتوسط

16.2 استخدام الطابق الأرضي	☑ للسكن 162م2 ☐ للعمل ☐ مظلة ☐ أخرى م2

17.2 استخدام منطقة العمل قبل العمل	☐ مستعملة من المالك ☐ خالية ☐ مستأجره	18.2 تشطيب منطقة العمل /المظلة	☐ فاخر ☐ غير مشطب ☐ متوسط ☐ تحت المتوسط

19.2 ملاحظات عامة

• نفيد بأن العائلة مستقلة عن أسر أخرى داخل الملكية "شقة مشروع بون اصص"

20.2 يرفق ما أمكن صورة عن كل من المستندات التالية مع وضع إشارة x على المستندات المرفقة :

☑ صورة الهوية	☐ إثبات ملكية الأرض	☑ رخصة البلدية	☐ أخرى .....

التوقيع: المهندس: يارب كمال المهندس: المهندس: أ.ج. نجار ممثل البلدية: منسق التدقيق: مسؤول المديرية:
التوقيع: التوقيع: التوقيع: التوقيع: التوقيع:

N4005-02

District/Municipality: North/Beit Lahya. Neighbourhood: Al-Ribat street/ Al-Ribat. Date of destruction: 29 12 2008. Method of destruction: direct strike. Date of inspection: 16 04 2009. State of building: total destruction. Floor area: 162 sqm. Type of building: residential. Number of units: 5. Number of units inhabited when destroyed: 5. Name of owner: Issam Mohammad Ismae'l Ali Salim, his brothers and mother. General remarks: the land on which the building was constructed was given in exchange for another piece of land and there is no official ownership documents provided. The building is 'part of Beit Lahya project'. Documents attached: photocopy of IDs, municipality building licence.

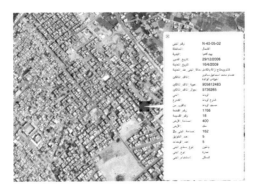

N2012-10. District/municipality: North/Beit Hanon. Date of destruction: 04 01 2009. Method of destruction: bulldozing. Date of inspection: 14 04 2009. State of building: completely destroyed. Floor area: 154 sqm. Type of building: industrial. Number of units: 1.

N3003-118. District/municipality: North/Jabaliya. Date of destruction: 09 01 2009. Method of destruction: bulldozing. Date of inspection: 05 05 2009. State of building: rubble. Floor area: 510 sqm. Type of building: residential. Number of units: 5.

N3003-121. District/municipality: North/Jabaliya neighbourhood. Date of destruction: 09 01 2009. Method of destruction: bulldozing. Date of inspection: 06 05 2009. State of the building: rubble. Floor area: 330 sqm. Type of building: residential. Number of units: 6. Number of units inhabited when destroyed: 6.

N4022-05. District/municipality: North/Beit Lahya. Date of destruction: 07 01 2009. Method of destruction: direct strike. Date of inspection: 14 04 2009. State of the building: total distruction. Floor area: 192 sqm. Type of building: residential. Number of units: 1. Number of units inhabited when destroyed: 1.

N3003-41. District/municipality: North/Jabaliya. Date of destruction: 08 01 2009. Method of destruction: bulldozing. Date of inspection: 20 04 2009. State of building: rubble. Floor area: 532 sqm. Type of building: industrial, Al-Mutawasit Concrete Factory. Number of units: 1. General remarks: land is owned by Ali family. Building has electricity only paid by factory. Water pool (9x8x6 m) attached to building.

N3004-101. District/municipality: North/Jabaliya. Date of destruction: 15 01 2009. Method of destruction: bulldozing. Date of inspection: 29 04 2009. State of building: rubble. Floor area: 220 sqm. Type of building: residential. Number of units: 1.

G1015-09. District/municipality: Gaza/Gaza City. Date of destruction: 05 01 2009. Method of destruction: bulldozing. Date of inspection: 21 04 2009. State of building: rubble. Floor area: 380 sqm. Type of building: residential. Number of units: 4.

G1049-01. District/municipality: Gaza/Gaza City. Date of destruction: 09 01 2009. Method of destruction: direct bombing. Date of inspection: 09 05 2009. State of building: fully destroyed. Floor area: 180 sqm. Type of building: residential. Number of units: 5.

G1014-07. District/municipality: Gaza/Gaza City. Date of destruction: 05 01 2009. Method of destruction: direct bombing. Date of inspection: 23 04 2009. State of building: rubble. Floor area: 160 sqm. Type of building: residential. Number of units: 3.

G1021-04. District/municipality: Gaza/Gaza City. Date of destruction: 13 01 2009. Method of destruction: bulldozing. Date of inspection: 16 04 2009. State of building: rubble. Floor area: 170 sqm. Type of building: residential. Number of units: 1.

K2002-03. District/municipality: Khan Younis. Date of destruction: 05 01 2009. Method of destruction: bulldozing. Date of inspection: 29 04 2009. State of building: rubble. Floor area: 150 sqm. Type of building: residential. Number of units: 1. General remarks: the construction beams for first floor were ready.

R1010-02. District/municipality: Rafah/Rafah City. Date of destruction: 05 01 2009. Method of destruction: nearby shelling. Date of inspection: 15 04 2009. State of building: fully destroyed. Floor area: 145 sqm. Type of building: residential. Number of units: 1.

N2003-02

N3003-94

N3003-95

N3003-96

N3003-98

N3003-100

N3003-106

N3003-122

N3003-130

N3004-93

N3004-110

N3004-111

N3004-113

G1014-01

G1015-19

G10177-01

G1021-02

G1021-08

G1022-02

G1049-02

K2001-02

K2002-02

K2002-03

K6001-01

160

K6001-02

K6001-08

K6002-10

K6002-11

R1002-03

R1008-01

R1008-03

R1008-10

R1008-11

R1008-27

R1009-02

R1009-31

Acknowledgements

Books often contain the idea-seeds that grow into their successors. *Hollow Land,* my previous book, ended with the problem of the lesser evil: the moderation and minimization of violence as a mechanism of government and control. *The Least of All Possible Evils* is an attempt to better understand this problem and its political consequences. For this purpose, minor characters to the plot of *Hollow Land* have here been made protagonists. They are not the architects of colonization and urban war; mostly, they are those well-meaning practitioners that seek to alleviate the pain caused by the latter but end up caught in power's grip, and often indvertently as its servants. It took a few years to help these characters up over the footnote line, eventually placing humanitarians and human rights workers in the arena of contemporary conflicts as full participants. Similarly, a new set of characters – forensic experts and gravediggers, scientists and sometimes fetishists, mentioned in passing here – now slowly grow to occupy centre stage in a new project I have just begun.

The Least of All Possible Evils, like its predecessor, has emerged out of an exhibition. The installation *665:The Lesser Evil* was a multiple screen work included in Manifesta 7, a European Biennial that took place on that occasion in Trento, Italy, within a section curated by Anselm Franke and Hila Peleg. The work was later exhibited in the context of the Spaport Biennial in Banja Luka, Bosnia-Herzegovina, in 2009 in a section curated, once again, by Franke. A pocket-size book based on some texts from the exhibition and translated and edited by Nicola Perugini, was published by the committed Italian publishers *Nottetempo* in 2009, thanks to the support of Ginevra Bompiani.

In preparation for this exhibition, I organized with Thomas Keenan and Eyal Sivan the workshop *Lesser Evils* at Bard College, New York, in February 2008. Its participants included Ariella Azoulay, Roger Berkowitz, Simon Critchley, Olivia Custer, Adi Ophir, Renata Salecl, Joshua Simon and Karen Sullivan. There was much in the discussion that took place at Bard College to inspire the work for Manifesta, and later, this book. For several months, Eyal Sivan and I worked on a joint contribution to the Manifesta exhibition, but this cooperation did not lead to a common project. I have, however, benefited from the discussions we had during the period of our collaboration and am grateful for the help he offered at the end, especially in preparation for the interview with Rony Brauman, and his advice on editing the video interviews, and even in physically building the installation in Trento. Ariella Azoulay and Adi Ophir, each in her and his own way, have been an important influence and a source of frequent support. Material generated by the program run by Adi Ophir and Michal Givoni, 'Catastrophe in the Making: Humanitarian Conditions in the Occupied Palestinian Territories', at Van Leer, Jerusalem, between 2004 and 2007, has also been a constant source of inspiration. DAAR, *Decolonizing Architecture/Art Residency* – the Beit Sahour–based architectural collective in which I am a founding member with Sandi Hilal and Alessandro Petti – provided a practical laboratory to discuss and investigate many of the ideas in this book. Eitan Diamond, quoted in these pages a few times throughout, is an inspiring humanitarian lawyer, successfully combing critical theory and legal practice. He has also read and suggested corrections to the text, especially on legal matters. Diamond, I must add, is also a close family relation. Lisa Hajjar has proposed the term 'humanitarian present' – in the context of the Mansour Armaly-IPS Panel of Palestine at the Middle East Studies Association (MESA) annual conference in Washington DC in 2011 that we organized around themes similar to those here. Ines Weizman, my partner, helped frame the project throughout and also gave the book its last major conceptual and structural push. The friend mentioned in Chapter 1 is the artist/theorist Florian Schneider. In more sense than one then this book should read like my part in a conversation between friends.

David Cunningham, Joan Copjec, Lieven De Cauter, Stefano Harney, Sina Najafi, Nicola Perugini, Alessandro Petti, Adrian Rifkin, Irit Rogoff, Albert Toscano, Susan Schuppli, Adania Shibli, Hito Steyerl, Paulo Tavares, members and students at the Centre for Research Architecture and colleagues at the Department of Visual Cultures at Goldsmiths helped on different aspects of the work. Emilio Distretti was my research assistant on this project and a virtual partner in its making. Tom Penn, my editor at Verso, has been, as always, my most attentive reader. In this case he was also the person that initiated the book by suggesting that it might be a good idea to 'write up' the Manifesta installation, and gracefully tolerated my delays in delivering the manuscript. I am, however, most indebted to my friend Thomas Keenan, who has had the largest influence on this work. He has helped shape my understanding of the contemporary problems and political stakes of humanitarianism and human rights and his advice and insight is reflected in virtually every aspect of this work.

Together with Carles Guerra, Tom also curated the exhibition *Antiphotojournalism* at La Virreina Center for the Image in Barcelona in June 2010 and at the FOAM in Amsterdam in March 2011. The exhibition provided me with the opportunity to collaborate with architects and friends Yazan Khalili and Tony Chakar in assembling the archive of destroyed buildings in Gaza.

The book includes material researched in the context of the ERC-funded project Forensic Architecture and is in fact one of the first products of this amazingly generous grant. The design and production of this book was funded by another grant kindly provided by the indispensable Graham Foundation for Advanced Studies in the Fine Arts.

Notes

1. The Humanitarian Present

1 Voltaire, *Candide, or Optimism*, trans. Theo Cuffe, London: Penguin Books, 2005, 13.
2 Sharon Sliwinski, 'The Aesthetics of Human Rights', *Culture, Theory & Critique*, 2009, 50(1), 23–39.
3 Leibniz's *Essays on the Goodness of God, the Freedom of Man and the Origin of Evil* was written in 1710.
4 Thanks to Hito Steyerl for this illuminating point.
5 Gottfried Wilhelm Leibniz, 'Discourse on Metaphysics', trans. George R. Montgomery, first published in Leibniz, Open Court Publishing Company, 1902. The translation was revised by Albert R. Chandler in 1924.
6 Giorgio Agamben, *The Kingdom and the Glory: For a Theological Genealogy of Economy and Government*, Stanford, CA: Stanford University Press, 2011.
7 John Rawls, 'Justice as Fairness: Political not Metaphysical,' *Philosophy and Public Affairs*, 14, no. 3 (1985): 233-51.
8 Adi Ophir called these things 'moral technologies', in the sense that they are techniques and structures configured in response to a moral demand to minimize the bad things in the world: 'these technologies were moral … because they involve the concrete, technical and material embodiment of compassion, mercy, pity, and sacrifice for the sake of others.' Adi Ophir, 'The Contribution of Global Humanitarianism to the Transformation of Sovereignty', roundtable.kein.org/node and in Adi Ophir, 'The Politics of Catastrophization', roundtable.kein.org/node/1094
9 Sliwinski, 'Aesthetics of Human Rights', 23–39.
10 Michel Foucault, *Security, Territory, Population: Lectures at the College de France 1977–1978*, ed. Arnold I. Davidson, trans. Graham Burchell, London: Palgrave Macmillan, 2007, 164–73, 183.
11 Michael Ignatieff, *The Lesser Evil: Political Ethics in an Age of Terror*, Princeton: Princeton University Press, 2004.
12 Ibid., xiv.
13 These refer respectively to *jus in bello* and *jus ad bellum*.
14 A former Israeli military lawyer Gabriella Blum opines that if international humanitarian law 'is designed to minimize humanitarian suffering within the constraints of war, then it is not at all clear why measures intended to further minimize suffering … a choice for

the lesser evil – cannot serve as a justification', she says effortlessly, 'for suspending the law in the name of the law'. Gabriella Blum, 'The Laws of War and the "Lesser Evil"', 35 YJIL 1 (2010), 3.

15 Relying on what is essentially a proportionality analysis, the Israeli Commission of Inquiry into the Methods of Investigation of the General Security Service Regarding Hostile Terrorist Activity, otherwise known as the Landau Commission, of 1987 reaches the conclusion that the prohibition on torture is not absolute, but is rather based, in its own words, upon the logic of 'the lesser evil'. Thus, 'the harm done by violating a provision of the law during an interrogation must be weighed against the harm to the life or person of others which could occur sooner or LATER' [upper-case in the original]. US Department of Justice attorney John Yoo similarly referred to a balance of interests when authorizing forms of torture during the Bush Administration. Itamar Mann and Omer Shatz, '"The Necessity Procedure: Laws of Torture in Israel and Beyond, 1987–2009', Legalleft, 2011, legalleft.org/wp-content/uploads/2011/02/2-necessity_procedure.pdf.

16 Ibid., 3.

17 Adi Ophir, *The Order of Evils: Toward an Ontology of Morals*, trans. Rela Mazali and Havi Carel, New York: Zone Books, 2005, section 7.100, 339; sections 7.2 and 7.3, 327–29. First published in Hebrew with Am Oved (Tel Aviv 2000). See, also, for example, section 7.335, 375.

18 Martti Koskenniemi, 'Human Rights Mainstreaming as a Strategy for Institutional Power', *Humanity: An International Journal of Human Rights, Humanitarianism, and Development*, vol. 1, no. 1, Fall 2010: 47–58; quote from 48–49. On the abuse of the proportionality princple see Aeyal M. Gross, 'The Construction of a Wall between The Hague and Jerusalem: The Enforcement and Limits of Humanitarian Law and the Structure of Occupation', *Leiden Journal of International Law*, 19 (2006): 393–440.

19 *Jus ad bellum* proportionality focuses on whether the overall legitimate objectives of a war are outweighed by the total damage (to civilians as well as military objectives) anticipated. *Jus in bello* proportionality, in contrast, is much narrower; it focuses on specific attacks during the campaign, and asks whether the incidental civilian deaths, or the incidental damage to civilian objects caused unintentionally in the process of attacking legitimate military objectives, outweigh the military advantages anticipated as a result of the specific attack.

20 Protocol Additional to the Geneva Conventions of 12 August 1949, and relating to the Protection of Victims of International Armed Conflicts (Protocol I), 8 June 1977.

21 Yotam Feldman, *The Lab*, Channel 8 films (Israel) 2011. Ben Israel: 'There is a mathematical formula that allows us to measure the amount of components within a system that we need to target in order for it to lose its information and collapse … the optimal is around the 20–25 per cent … for the entire system to collapse. Out of the list of terrorists that conduct operations about 20–25 were hit and their system collapsed in the West Bank'.

22 For proportionality analysis in areas where a military has effective control or feels it can commit to ground operation and can conduct ground operation for the purpose of an arrest, say, the calculus is different from that in which a military does not have such control, and chooses to conduct a targeted operation with civilian casualties.

23 Daniel Reisner interviewed by Eyal Weizman by telephone, London to Tel Aviv, 15 December 2010.

24 Ronald C. Arkin, 'Ethical Robots in Warfare', *Technology Research News*, 9 December 2005. See also Armin Krishnan, *Killer Robots: Legality and Ethicality of Autonomous Weapons*, Ashgate: Surrey, 2009.

25 Eitan Diamond in conversation, 11 February 2011.

26 David Kennedy, *The Dark Sides of Virtue: Reassessing International Humanitarianism*, Princeton, NJ: Princeton University Press, 2004, 235–323.

27 The manual is here: fas.org/irp/doddir/army/fm3-24fd.pdf

28 Sarah Sewall, Introduction, *The U.S. Army/Marine Corps Counterinsurgency Field Manual*, Chicago: University of Chicago Press, 2007.

29 Initial United States Forces – Afghanistan (USFOR-A) Assessment Commanders Summary, globalsecurity.org/military/library/report/2009/090830-afghan-assessment/090830-afghan-assessment-01.htm. This was also sourced by a Pentagon programme, called the Human Terrain System, which employed anthropologists in research with the idea that the military should have a deeper understanding of the cultures and societies in which it conducts its counterinsurgency campaigns. Defense Secretary Robert Gates has said, 'The net effect of these efforts is often less violence across the board and fewer hardships and civilian deaths.' Patricia Cohen, 'Panel Criticizes Military's Use of Embedded Anthropologists', *New York Times*, 3 December 2009.

30 'Rather than a giant computer game, modern war turned out to be more like social work with guns.' Andrew Bacevich, 'Social Work with Guns', *London Review of Books*, vol. 31, no. 24, 17 December 2009. See also Tom Hayden, 'Kilcullen's Long War', *The Nation*, 2 November 2009.

31 'Once a specific crime has appeared for the first time, its reappearance is more likely than its initial emergence could ever have been.' Hannah Arendt, Epilogue, *Eichmann in Jerusalem: A Report on the Banality of Evil*, Penguin: Harmondsworth, 1963, 273. Philosopher Alexander Duttmann termed this the potentiality of the worst. Alexander García Düttmann, 'The Worst, the Better and the Lesser of Two Evils. Some Thoughts on Revolution and Literature', lecture at Goldsmiths, University of London, 19 October 2010.

32 Even in its negation – articulated in the use of the term 'disproportionate' – the reference to the law is invoked. Human rights scholar Thomas Keenan offers a more subtle interpretation about the relation between law and violence. Being in control and out of control, upholding and violating international law, are not diametric opposites. Rather, they are complementary actions undertaken in relation to the law, and demonstrate the power of international humanitarian law to condition the battlefield as a discursive field. Disproportionality is thus a relation between violence and law that is more complex than mere disregard. The threat of projecting force in excess of calculations resonates precisely because it has been articulated against the backdrop of the legal principles of proportionality. Disproportionality affirms the law in its violation. Thomas Keenan, 'Going Wild: Language, War, and Translation', paper given at Excess of Order, Pericentre, Cairo, January 2010.

33 Gabriel Siboni, 'Disproportionate Force: Israel's Concept of Response in Light of the Second Lebanon War', INSS Insight No. 74, October 2, 2008. After the end of the Gaza attack Prime Minister Ehud Olmert explained that this doctrine would become Israel's guiding principle in future wars: 'Our response will be *disproportionate*. We won't go back to the rules that the terrorist organizations tried to dictate.' Israel Channel 2 News, 1 February 2009 (in Hebrew). Available at: mako.co.il/news-military/security/Article-34a141791e03f11004.htm

The Goldstone report also insisted that Israel waged 'a deliberately disproportionate attack designed to punish, humiliate and terrorize a civilian population, radically diminish its local economic capacity both to work and to provide for itself, and to force upon it an ever-increasing sense of dependency and vulnerability.'

34 Vladimir Lenin, 'Left-Wing Communism: An Infantile Disorder', April–May 1920. Trotsky defended the same principles in 'The Third International after Lenin' (1928): 'Purely practical agreements can be concluded with the devil himself, if that

is advantageous at a given moment. But it would be absurd in such a case to demand that the devil should generally become converted to Christianity, and that he use his horns … for pious deeds. In presenting such conditions, we act in reality as the devil's advocates, and beg him to let us become his godfathers.'

35 Robert Pirsig, *Zen and the Art of Motorcycle Maintenance*, New York: Bantam Books, 1974.

2. Arendt in Ethiopia

1 Hannah Arendt, *Responsibility and Judgment*, New York: Schocken Books, 2003, 36–7.

2 'Learning from Dilemmas', Rony Brauman interviewed by Michel Feher and Philippe Mangeot, 131–47, in Michel Feher, ed., *Nongovernmental Politics*, New York: Zone Books, 2007, 141.

3 In a series of BBC reports in March 2010, a former TPLF fighter described masquerading as a Sudanese merchant and selling bags of 'grain' – containing sand – to the aid workers, who then passed the sacks on to other TPLF cadres, who returned them to the 'Sudanese traders,' who resold them to the aid workers, and so on. In this way, bags of grain/sand circulated back and forth across the border, as money poured into TPLF coffers.

4 Pascal Bruckner, 'Tiers-Monde, culpabilité, haine de soi', Rony Brauman, Fondation Liberté sans Frontières, eds., *Le Tiers-mondisme en question*, Paris: O. Orban, 1986. Pascal Bruckner, *The Tears of the White Man: Compassion as Contempt*, New York: The Free Press, 1986 (1983).

5 Rony Brauman interviewed by Eyal Weizman at MSF offices, Paris, 21 May 2008.

6 Ibid.

7 Ibid.

8 A famine is measured by widespread statistical rates of hunger, malnutrition and mortality. The UN now defines famine as an intake of 1,500 calories or less a day (compared with the minimum standard of 2,100 a day), water consumption of less than four litres a day and a mortality rate of more than 2 people per 10,000 per day.

9 MSF archive, consulted on 21 May 2008.

10 Conor Foley, *The Thin Blue Line*, London: Verso: 2008, 168–9.

11 MSF archive, consulted on 21 May 2008.

12 All quotes in this paragraph are from Brauman in interview, May 2008.

13 Alex de Waal, *Famine Crimes: Politics & the Disaster Relief Industry in Africa*, Oxford: James Currey and the International African Institute, 1997, 107.

14 MSF archive.

15 MSF archive.

16 Raul Hilberg, *The Destruction of the European Jews*, 1973 (1961), 122–5.

17 Totalitarians, according to Arendt, use the 'lesser evil' argument to camouflage their radical acts from unwitting participants, or from those yet to be initiated – the majority of bourgeois subjects needed to run things until a 'new man' was created – and even from their victims. Seeking to force the subject into compliance, they merely pose a set of alternatives in such a way that free subjects, choosing the lesser evil in pursuit of their interest, will end up serving the aims of the regime. In her essay 'The Eggs Speak Up', a witty reference to Stalin's dictum that 'you can't make an omelette without breaking a few eggs', Arendt pleaded for 'a radical negation of the whole concept of lesser evil in politics'. Hannah Arendt, 'The Eggs Speak Up' (1950), Jerome Kohn, ed., *Essays in Understanding, 1930–1954: Formation, Exile, and Totalitarianism*, New York: Schocken Books, 2005.

18 Rony Brauman and Eyal Sivan, *Adolf Eichmann: The Nazi Criminal Who Organized the Destruction of the Jewish People*, Torino: Einaudi, 2003. (Emilio Distretti, who was my research assistant on this project, has translated some relevant paragraphs of this book from the Italian version.)

19 Brauman in interview, May 2008. This position has received some support from Bob Geldof, who went so far as to claim, 'The resettlement programme would [have continued] whether or not we chose to help, just as Hitler's extermination of the Jews would have continued whether or not aid workers had contrived to help alleviate the sufferings in the camps. … Our work [in Ethiopia] employed the same argument.' See David Rieff, 'The Humanitarian Aid Industry's Most Absurd Apologist', *New Republic*, 29 November 2010.

20 Brauman in interview, May 2008.

21 Bernard-Henri Lévy, *Left in Dark Times*, New York: Random House, 2008, 70.

22 Judith Shklar, 'The Liberalism of Fear', Nancy L. Rosenbaum, ed., *Liberalism and the Moral Life*, Cambridge, MA: Harvard University Press, 1989. For Shklar, a focus on hope, utopia or the good might make us forget the evils of modernism, which persist in all forms of unrestrained government cruelty.

23 In relation to Arendt's evaluation of the Holocaust in her famous quote to the effect that 'once a specific crime has appeared for the first time, its reappearance is more likely than its initial emergence could ever have been' – the philosopher Alexander Duttmann called it 'the potentiality of the worst'. The worst necessarily creates a precedent against which all other bad events are understood, compared, measured and evaluated – gauging a constantly variable distance from it. Hannah Arendt, *Eichmann in Jerusalem: A Report on the Banality of Evil*, 1963 (Epilogue). Alexander García Düttmann, 'The Worst, the Better and the Lesser of Two Evils. Some Thoughts on Revolution and Literature': lecture at Goldsmiths, University of London, 19 October 2010. The declaration against genocide (a term for the structural universalizing of the Holocaust and its inscription in a universal code) after the end of WWII with its scales from 1 to 8, was itself an attempt to provide a gradient to measure this distance.

24 Daniel Levy and Natan Sznaider, 'The Institutionalization of Cosmopolitan Morality: The Holocaust and Human Rights', *Journal of Human Rights*, vol. 3, no. 2 June 2004: 143–57.

25 Rony Brauman, ed., *Le Tiers-mondisme en Question*, Paris: O. Orban, 1986.

26 MSF archives.

27 Edward Said, 'Always on Top', *London Review of Books* vol. 25. no. 6, 20 March 2003.

28 Hannah Arendt, *The Origins of Totalitarianism*, New York: Harcourt, Brace, Jovanovich, 1973.

29 Brauman in interview, May 2008.

30 James Rosenau, *Turbulence in World Politics*, New York: Harvester Wheatsheaf, 1990.

31 The famous BBC broadcast from Korem on 23 October 1984 opens with the following words, spoken by Michael Buerk over misty atmospheric shots of daybreak: 'Dawn, and as the sun breaks through the piercing chill of night on the plain outside Korem, it lights up a biblical famine, now, in the twentieth century. This place, say workers here, is the closest thing to Hell on earth. Thousands of wasted people … flood in every day from villages hundreds of miles away, felled by hunger, driven to the point of desperation…' in de Waal, *Famine Crimes*, 121–2.

32 Stuart Hall and Martin Jacques, 'PEOPLE AID: A New Politics Sweeps the Land', *Marxism Today*, 10 July 1986: 121–2.

33 Bob Geldof: 'That criticism irritates me, but then I think it makes people question even further: what price criticism when the end result of a bunch of people in the studio is without doubt the end result of millions of people being helped to stay alive?', *Rolling Stone*, 12 May 1985.

34 Bob Geldof interviewed for *Le Monde*, 11 December 1986.

35 Michal Givoni, 'The Advent of the Emergency: Political Theory and Humanitarian Expertise', paper delivered the Conference 'Power, Rule and Governmentality in Zones of Emergency: The Israeli Occupation in a Global Perspective', Van Leer Institute, Jerusalem, 3–5 June 2007; and Michal Givoni, 'Witnessing in Action: Ethics and Politics in a World Without Borders', later published in Adi Ophir, Michal Givoni, Sari Hanafi, *Power of Inclusive Exclusion*, New York: Zone Books, 2009.

36 François Bugnion, *The International Committee of the Red Cross and the Protection of War Victims*, Oxford: Macmillan Press and the International Committee of the Red Cross, 2003.

37 Luc Boltanski, *Distant Suffering: Morality, Media and Politics*, Cambridge: Cambridge University Press, 1999. This is how MSF has puts the issue of witnessing on its own Web site: 'In carrying out humanitarian assistance … MSF acts as a witness and will speak out, either in private or in public about the plight of populations in danger'.

38 Didier Fassin, 'The Humanitarian Politics of Testimony: Subjectification through Trauma in the Israeli–Palestinian Conflict,' *Cultural Anthropology*, vol. 23, Issue 3: 531–58.

39 Ibid.

40 This dynamic is beautifully unpacked in Eric Stover, *The Witnesses: War Crimes and the Promise of Justice in The Hague*, Philadelphia: University of Pennsylvania Press, 2005.

41 Rony Brauman interviewed by Eyal Weizman, 29 September 2010 (by telephone).

42 Interview with Rony Brauman, *Paris Match*, 14 November 85.

43 Although the report contained strong allegations, confirming that more than two hundred thousand people had died and crimes against humanity were perpetrated, it was immediately used by the Bachir government to exonerate itself.

44 Brauman in interview, September 2010.

45 Brauman in interview, May 2008.

46 Kouchner left MSF due to a conflict of opinion with Brauman and MSF's chairman, Claude Malhuret, and formed Médecins du Monde in 1980.

47 UN Resolution 43/131 was passed on 8 December 1988.

48 On 16 September 2005, the UN General Assembly adopted a resolution with Paragraphs 138 and 139 dealing with the 'responsibility to protect populations from genocide, war crimes, ethnic cleansing and crimes against humanity'.

49 Pierre Péan, *Le Monde selon K.*, Paris: Fayard, 2009.

50 Ron Paul (Republican member of Congress from Texas), US House of Representatives, 23 July 2004, 3 August 2004.

51 Mahmood Mamdani, *Saviors and Survivors: Darfur, Politics, and the War on Terror*, London: Verso: 2009, 4, 22, 56, 58.

52 Bernard-Henri Lévy, 'SOS Darfur!', *Huffington Post*, 11 January 2010.

53 Andrew Anthony, 'Does Humanitarian Aid Prolong Wars?', *Observer*, 25 April 2010.

54 Secretary of State Colin Powell, Remarks to the National Foreign Policy Conference for Leaders of Nongovernmental Organizations, 26 October 2001.

55 David Rieff, 'How NGOs Became Pawns in the War on Terrorism', *New Republic*, 3 August 2010.

56 Brauman, 'Learning from Dilemmas', 136.

57 During the other prominent crises of the 1990s his pronouncements and actions called for humanitarianism to be positioned away from militaries – Western or otherwise. During the war in Somalia it was about the militarization of the 'humanitarian mission' that ended up shooting many of the people it came to protect. Several months after the massacres in Rwanda it was about the way the Hutu militias that undertook them were using international aid in order to regroup and use the refugee camps as rear bases for guerilla action. He equally protested the way in which Rwandan and Burundian forces used humanitarian aid as bait to capture other Hutu refugees in Zaire.

58 Brauman in interview, September 2010.

59 See especially Michel Agier, *On the Margins of the World: The Refugee Experience Today*, trans. David Fernbach, London: Polity, 2008.

60 Eyal Weizman and Rony Brauman in conversation, Columbia University, 4 February 2008.

61 Brauman, 'Learning from Dilemmas', 141.

62 Ignatieff, *The Lesser Evil: Political Ethics in an Age of Terror*.

63 Brauman in interview, September 2010.

64 David Rieff, *A Bed for the Night: Humanitarianism in Crisis*, London: Vintage, 2002.

65 As David Rieff puts it 'Those who have played Luther to the Red Cross's Rome were, it seemed, more and more ready to heal the schism.' David Rieff, *A Bed for the Night*, 331.

66 ICRC, 'Components and Bodies of the International Movement of the Red Cross and Red Crescent'. See: icrc.org

67 'MSF's Principles and Identity: The Challenges Ahead', MSF International Activity Report, 2005, doctorswithoutborders.org

68 Michel Agier, 'The Undesirables of the World and How Universality Changed Camp', 16 May 2011, opendemocracy.net

69 Agier, *On the Margins of the World*, 60.

70 This would exclude situations such as the one in Ethiopia, where the Ethiopian military participated in relief and feeding centres; or in Kosovo and Afghanistan where humanitarians worked alongside NATO forces; or following the genocide in Rwanda, where aid agencies were present in camps under the control of Hutu Power militias in Goma.

71 Rony Brauman interviewed by Eyal Weizman, 20 December 2010.

72 Rony Brauman, *L'Humanitaire, le Dilemme: Entretiens avec Philippe Petite*, Paris: Editions Textuel, 1996, 43–44.

73 Brauman in interview, September 2010.

74 Givoni, 'The Advent of the Emergency'.

75 Agier, 'The Undesirables of the World'.

76 Manuel Herz, 'Refugee Camps or Ideal Cities in Dust and Dirt', in Ilka and Andreas Ruby (eds), Urban Trans Formations, Berlin: Ruby Press, 2008.

77 Alex de Waal, 'Whose Emergency Is It Anyway? Dreams, Tragedies and Traumas in the Humanitarian Encounter', roundtable.kein.org/node/1078

78 Rony Brauman, 'From Philanthropy to Humanitarianism: Remarks and an Interview', *The South Atlantic Quarterly*, vol. 103, no. 2/3, Spring/Summer 2004: 397–417.

79 Michel Agier, 'Humanity as an Identity and Its Political Effects (A Note on Camps and Humanitarian Government)', in *Humanity*, Fall 2010, 29.

80 Michel Agier in conversation at a seminar at the Centre for Research Architecture, 7 October 2011.

81 Thomas Keenan, 'Tidying Up', a lecture delivered at the conference Sovereignty and Bare Life: Zones of Conflict, 29 November 2008, Tate Modern, London.

3. The Best of All Possible Walls

1 Ludwig Wittgenstein, *Notebooks 1914–1916*, G. H. von Wright and G. E. M. Anscombe, eds., trans. G. E. M. Anscombe, Chicago: University of Chicago Press, 1979, 7e.

2 HCJ 2056/04 *Beit Sourik Village Council v. The Government of Israel*, 58(5) P.D. 807 (2004). *Legal Consequences of the Construction of a Wall in the Occupied Palestinian Territory* (Advisory Opinion), Judgment of 9 July 2004 (2004).

3 See adalah.org/eng

4 The strategy of Adalah was defined in terms that are similar to those of the legendary French lawyer Jacques Vergès. The latter's 'strategy of rupture' uses the courts and instruments of the law to delegitimize its basis, putting the very system on trial.

5 Muhammad Dahla interviewed by Eyal Weizman at his office, Jerusalem, 17 June 2008.

6 Gadi Ma-Tov interviewed by Eyal Weizman at his studio, Jerusalem, 17 June 2008.

7 Gadi Ma-Tov, 17 June 2008.

8 The PSC defines itself as a 'voluntary body with no party political affiliation ... with a solid background in fields associated with security and diplomacy ... considering Peace to be a necessary component of Israeli National Security.' peace-security-council.org

9 Dahla in interview, June 2008.

10 Ibid.

11 Shuli Hartman in email correspondence, August 2007.

12 'Because they could materialize and articulate the different kinds of knowledge ... models were a common medium of argumentation, and in demonstrations they animated, complicated, and in some sense eclipsed textual descriptions and drawings.' Alain Pottage and Brad Sherman, *Figures of Invention: A History of Modern Patent Law*, Oxford: Oxford University Press, 2010.

13 HCJ 2056/04 *Beit Sourik*.

14 Amos Harel, 'Chief of Staff Ashkenazi: The Route of the Wall Is a Political Matter,' *Ha'aretz*, 28 July 2008.

15 'The HCJ's legal analysis involves a misplaced transplantation of proportionality doctrines developed in international and domestic law into the occupation context, leading to an imbalanced rights/security equation ... The use of this administrative principle in the context of a military occupation is particularly problematic. When used to review administrative action, the principle of proportionality assumes an accountable democratic government committed to the collective good of its citizens, but occasionally forced to violate the rights of part or the whole population in order to attain legitimate ends. The benefits to the population are then weighed against the infringement of their rights, the point being that the benefits accrue to the *same* population whose rights were violated.' Aeyal M. Gross, 'The Construction of a Wall between The Hague and Jerusalem: The Enforcement and Limits of Humanitarian Law and the Structure of Occupation', *Leiden Journal of International Law* 19, 2006: 393–440.

16 Michael Sfard interviewed by Eyal Weizman at his office, Tel Aviv, 19 June 2008. He also said, 'If we keep on referring to a speculative *greater evil* that may occur as a consequence of our work we find ourselves ... sacrificing the individual. If a client comes to me and says that the route planned will completely cut off his livelihood because he has an olive grove and he asks for my help, I am bound professionally, ethically and definitively by human rights standards to do everything under the law to help this person protect their livelihood. And I should refer to the overall damage that the entire campaign is causing to the big cause of the Palestinian people as a whole.'

17 For a discussion of Michel Foucault's concept of an apparatus see Giorgio Agamben, *What Is an Apparatus?*, Stanford, CA: Stanford University Press, 2009, 8–11.

18 The envelope was reinforced along the Gaza perimeter fence, in the policing of the airspace above and the territorial waters in the west. The 'terminals' in the wall are located in Israeli territory, thus exclusively operated by it. Israel's control over the border crossings is extended to the Rafah crossing between Gaza and Egypt via agreements with Egypt, which participated in the enactment of the siege.

19 This is taken from the verdict. See HCJ 9132/07, Jaber Al-Bassiouni Ahmed and others v. 1. Prime Minister. 2. Minister of Defence 2007. mfa.gov.il/NR/rdonlyres/938CCD2E-89C7-4E77-B071-56772DFF79CC/0/HCJGazaelectricity.pdf

20 For the definition of hunger, see the Integrated Food Security Phase Classification,

ipcinfo.org. 'The Integrated Food Security Phase Classification (IPC) is a standardized tool that aims at providing a "common currency" for classifying food security.

Using a common scale, which is comparable across countries, will make it easier for donors, agencies and governments to identify priorities for intervention before they become catastrophic.'

21 Article 23 of the Fourth Geneva Convention of 1949 requires a party to a conflict to allow the free passage of goods intended for the citizens of the adverse party. Article 70 of the First Additional Protocol to the Geneva Conventions, of 1977, sets forth a broader obligation, whereby the parties to the conflict must allow the rapid and unimpeded passage of vital goods to the civilian population. See icrc.org/ihl.nsf/INTRO/470

22 HCJ 9132/07.

23 See, for one example, Jean Ziegler, 'The Right to Food, Addendum: Mission to the Occupied Palestinian Territories', UNISPAL document E/CN.4/2004/10/Add.2, 31 October 2003.

24 HCJ 9132/07.

25 Israel's Ministry for Foreign Affairs, 'Deputy Foreign Minister Ayalon: The Flotilla's Goal Is the Delegitimization of Israel', 29 May 2010. mfa.gov.il/MFA/About+the+Ministry/MFA+Spokesman/2010/The-flotillas-goal-is-the-delegitimization-of-Israel-29-May-2010.htm

26 HCJ 9132/07.

27 Yotam Feldman and Uri Blau, 'Gaza Bonanza,' Ha'aretz, 11 June 2009.

28 Joy Gordon, *Invisible War: The United States and the Iraq Sanctions*, Cambridge, MA: Harvard University Press, 2010; Peter Pellett, 'Sanctions, Food, Nutrition, and Health in Iraq', in Anthony Arnove, *Iraq under Siege: The Deadly Impact of Sanctions and War*, London: Pluto, 2003, 185–203.

29 David R. Francis, 'What Aid Cutoff to Hamas Would Mean', *Christian Science Monitor*, 27 February 2006. See note 20.

30 Feldman and Blau, 'Gaza Bonanza'.

31 IDF humanitarian coordination, 'An Interview with Baruch Spiegel', 19 February 2009, edition 7, vol. 7, bitterlemons-international.org/inside.php?id=1066

32 Ariella Azoulay, 'Hunger in Palestine: The Event That Never Was', in Anselm Franke, Rafi Segal, and Eyal Weizman, eds., *Territories, Islands, Camps and Other States of Utopia*, Cologne: Walter Koening, 2003, 154–7. See also Ilana Feldman, 'Gaza's Humanitarianism Problem,' *Journal of Palestine Studies* vol. XXXVIII, no. 3, Spring 2009: 22–37.

33 Darryl Li, 'Disengagement and the Frontiers of Zionism,' 16 February 2008, Middle East Report, merip.org/mero/mero021608.html

34 Adi Ophir, 'The Politics of Catastrophization,' Centre for Research Architecture, 1 February 2009, roundtable.kein.org/node/1094.

35 Yotam Feldman, 'Red Lines', *Mita'am*, May 2010.

36 Sari Hanafi, 'Spacio-cide: Colonial Politics, Invisibility and Rezoning in Palestinian Territory', *Contemporary Arab Affairs*, vol. 2, no. 1, 2009: 106–21.

37 However, this mode of counting and calculating mortality recently received a legal status when the ICC prosecutor Luis Moreno-Ocampo included it in the arrest warrant against Sudan's president, Omar el-Bashir, accusing the latter of deliberately using his minister for humanitarian affairs to control living conditions calculated to bring about the physical destruction of millions of people in the displaced persons camps of Darfur. Moreno-Ocampo accused Bashir of deliberately inflicting on the Fur, Masalit and Zaghawa ethnic groups living conditions calculated to bring about their physical destruction. Millions of Darfuris are living in camps of displaced persons. Ahmad Harun, Bashir's minister of state for the interior and later minister of state for humanitarian affairs, controlled genocidal conditions in the displaced persons' camps within

Sudan's control. In July 2010 the ICC in The Hague charged President Al-Bashir with three counts of genocide. Besides the 'genocide by killing and causing serious bodily harm', it introduced the category of 'genocide by deliberately inflicting conditions of life calculated to bring about physical destruction'. Luis Moreno-Ocampo, 'Now End This Darfur Denial', *Guardian*, 15 July 2010.

38 'Electricity Shortage in Gaza: Who Turned Out the Lights?', Gisha position paper, May 2010, gisha.org/UserFiles/File/publications/ElectricitypaperEnglish.pdf; Noga Kadman, 'Red Lines Crossed: Destruction of Gaza Infrastructure', Gisha position paper, August 2009, gisha.org/UserFiles/File/publications_/Infrastructures_Report_Aug09_Eng.pdf

39 Throughout November no more than 6 per cent of the minimum nutritional requirements entered through the terminals. There were three days in November when UNRWA, the main provider of nutrition, ran out of food altogether, with the result that on each of these days 20,000 people were unable to receive food. Sara Roy, 'If Gaza Falls …', *London Review of Books*, vol. 31, no. 1, 1 January 2009: 26.

40 Walter Benjamin, 'Critique of Violence', trans. Edmund Jephcott, in Peter Demetz, ed., *Reflections*, 1978, 283.

41 Eitan Diamond, 'Reshaping International Humanitarian Law to Suit the Ends of Power' at the conference Humanitarianism and International Humanitarian Law: Reflecting on Change over Time in Theory, Law, and Practice, held at the Law School, the College of Management Academic Studies in Rishon Lezion, 16–17 December 2009.

42 Charles J. Dunlap, 'Lawfare: A Decisive Element of 21st-Century Conflicts?', *Joint Force Quarterly* 3, 2009: 35. See also Charles J. Dunlap, 'Law and Military Interventions: Preserving Humanitarian Values in 21st-Century Conflicts', at the conference Humanitarian Challenges in Military Intervention, Carr Center for Human Rights Policy in the Kennedy School of Government, Harvard University, 29 November 2001. See also Charles Dunlap, 'Lawfare amid Warfare', *Washington Times*, 3 August 2007.

43 David Kennedy, *Of War and Law*, Princeton: Princeton University Press, 2006, 33.

44 Asa Kasher, 'A Moral Evaluation of the Gaza War', *Jerusalem Post*, 7 February 2010.

45 See Yotam Feldman and Uri Blau, 'Consent and Advise', *Ha'aretz*, 5 February 2009.

46 Ibid.

47 Asa Kasher, 'Operation Cast Lead and the Ethics of Just War', *Azure*, no. 37, summer, 2009: 43–75.

48 The military's 'international law division' and its operational branch have devised tactics that would allow soldiers to apply what might be called 'technologies of warning.' Delivered to homesteads by telephone or sometimes by warning shots, they aim to shift people between legal designations – as soon as a civilian picks up the phone in his home, his legal designation changes from an 'uninvolved civilian', protected by IHL, to a voluntary 'human shield' – from a subject to an object, a simple part of the architecture. Technologies of warning intervene in the legal categories of both 'distinction' and 'proportionality': with regard to the former, they transfer people from illegitimate to legitimate targets by forcing them into a legal category that is not protected; and with regard to the latter, they imply a different calculation of proportionality. Human shields are not designated as combatants but are not counted as uninvolved civilians in the calculations of proportionality which must assess damage against the life lost.

49 John Yoo, *The Powers of War and Peace*, Chicago: University of Chicago Press, 2005.

50 Itamar Mann and Omer Shatz, 'The Necessity Procedure: Laws of Torture in Israel and Beyond, 1987–2009', *Legalleft*, 2011, legalleft.org/wp-content/uploads/2011/02/2-necessity_procedure.pdf

51 Michael Sfard in a public lecture titled 'Accountability, Impunity, the Goldstone Report and the Role of Government Lawyers', which he delivered on 24 November 2009 at the

conference Securing Compliance with International Humanitarian Law: The Promise and Limits of Enforcement Mechanisms, in Jerusalem, 22–24 November 2009.

52 Some of these crimes were in fact investigated and prosecuted by the Israeli military's courts. Human Rights Watch, 'Witness Accounts and Additional Analysis of IDF Use of White Phosphorus', 25 March 2009, hrw.org/en/news/2009/03/25/witness-accounts-and-additional-analysis-idf-use-white-phosphorus

4. Forensic Architecture: Only the Criminal Can Solve the Crime

1 Cornelia Vismann, 'The Love of Ruins' *Perspectives on Science*, 2001, vol. 9, no. 2: 196.

2 Richard Goldstone et al., 'Report of the United Nations Fact Finding Mission on the Gaza Conflict', Human Rights Council, 15 September 2009 (hereafter the Goldstone report).

3 The HRW reports Garlasco contributed to (not on Israel – these will be discussed later): 'A Dying Practice: Use of Cluster Munitions by Russia and Georgia in August 2008', 2009; 'Troops in Contact: Airstrikes and Civilian Deaths in Afghanistan', 2008; 'Flooding South Lebanon: Israel's Use of Cluster Munitions in Lebanon in July and August 2006', 2008; '"No Blood, No Foul": Soldiers' Accounts of Detainee Abuse in Iraq', 2005; 'Leadership Failure: Firsthand Accounts of Torture of Iraqi Detainees by the US Army's 82nd Airborne Division', 2005; 'Off Target: The Conduct of the War and Civilian Casualties in Iraq', 2003.

4 For earlier HRW reports on Israel see, for example, 'Razing Rafah: Mass Home Demolitions in the Gaza Strip', 17 September 2004; and 'Gaza Beach Investigation Ignores Evidence', 19 June 2006.

5 According to a list of names published by the Israeli human rights organization B'Tselem, the IDF operations killed 1,387 Palestinians, at least 762 of whom were civilians. Thirteen Israelis died during the fighting, three of them civilians. The UN Office for the Coordination of Humanitarian Affairs (OCHA) estimated that 3,914 buildings were completely destroyed, 21,000 housing units were destroyed or badly damaged and about 51,000 people were displaced. OCHA, 'Gaza Flash Appeal', February 2009, 1.

6 Omri Ceren, 'Marc Garlasco: Is HRW's Anti-Israel Investigator a Nazi-Obsessed Collector?', 8 September 2009. 'The leather SS jacket makes my blood go cold, it is so COOL!' Garlasco wrote in one of these collector forums.

7 'PM Netanyahu Addresses the Saban Forum', 15 November 2009, mfa.gov.il/MFA/Government/Speeches+by+Israeli+leaders/2009/PM_Netanyahu_addresses_Saban_Forum_15-Nov-2009.htm

8 Thomas Keenan and Eyal Weizman, 'Israel: The Third Strategic Threat', *openDemocracy*, 7 June 2010.

9 Dermer was quoted in Herb Keinon, 'Diplomacy: Israel vs. Human Rights Watch', *Jerusalem Post*, 16 July 2009.

10 The Goldstone report, 6–9. The commission included Desmond Travers, a retired colonel in the Irish military. 'I took the job not for HR or a moralistic reason … I have to be honest, it was the perfect case of two extremes – high technological army against an insurgency in a confined space and it lasted over three weeks – and that was a perfect model to study, and that is why I volunteered.' http://fora.tv/2011/05/19/Naomi_Klein_Blueprint_for_Accountability

11 Goldstone's work was to pave the way for the establishment of the Truth and Reconciliation Commission in 1995, a body that he strongly supported. Later allegations embroiled Goldstone in a controversy of his own when an Israeli newspaper revealed

that he signed the execution orders of at least twenty-eight black defendants when he was judged in South African under the Apartheid regime. See Tehiya Barak, 'Judge Goldstone's Dark Past', Ynet, 5 June 2010.

12 *Quintilian's Institutes of Oratory*, Book 9, Chapter 2.

13 Miguel Tamen, *Friends of Interpretable Objects*, Cambridge, MA: Harvard University Press, 2004, 79.

14 Jane Bennet, *Vibrant Matter: A Political Ecology of Things*, Durham and London: Duke University Press, 2010, 9.

15 Fernando Vidal, 'Miracles, Science, and Testimony in Post-Tridentine Saint-Making', *Science in Context*, vol. 20, no. 3, 2007: 481–508.

16 In the nineteenth century, photographs as courtroom evidence were often understood as pale substitutes for evidence, posing legal challenges and even being referred to as 'the hearsay of the sun.' Photographic images were banned from courts. But once entered, they still were treated with much suspicion and ultimately had to prove their status as reliable evidence. See: Joel Snyder, 'Res Ipsa Loquitur', Lorraine Daston, ed., *Things That Talk: Object Lessons from Art and Science*, New York, Zone Books, 2007.

17 Tamem, *Friends of Interpretable Objects*, 79.

18 This was the title of a series of seminars I taught with Thomas Keenan and Nikolaus Hirsch at the Stadel School in Frankfurt in the academic year 2010–11, staedelschule.de/forensic_aesthetics_d.html

19 David Stark and Verena Paravel, 'PowerPoint in Public: Digital Technologies and the New Morphology of Demonstration', *Theory, Culture & Society*, vol. 25, no. 5, September 2008: 30.

20 Christopher Joyce and Eric Stover, *Witnesses from the Grave: The Stories That Bones Tell*, Boston: Little, Brown and Company, 1991, 75.

21 Steven Byers, *Introduction to Forensic Anthropology: A Textbook*, Boston: Allyn & Bacon Publishers, 2002; John Hunter, Charlotte Roberts and Anthony Martin, eds., *Studies in Crime: Introduction to Forensic Archaeology*, London: Routledge, 1995; Margaret Cox and Simon Mays, eds., *Human Osteology: In Archaeology and Forensic Science*, Cambridge: Cambridge University Press, 2000.

22 Joyce and Stover, *Witnesses from the Grave*, 149–214. At about the same time, Snow, together with other members of the American Association for the Advancement of Science (AAAS), responded to requests from Argentinean organizations to help in the exhumation of unmarked graves containing the remains of the '*desaparecidos*', the 'disappeared' killed by the Argentinean military regime in the Dirty War of 1976–83.

23 Thomas Keenan and Eyal Weizman in conversation, ArteEast/Parsons School of Design, 13 February 2010.

24 Quoted in Dario A. Euraque, 'The Science of Forensic Anthropology and Human Rights in the Americas', trincoll.edu/orgs/scialnce/SFR/01-02/Files/Forensic%20 Anthropology.doc

25 In the context of the Kosovo Cultural Heritage Project, carried out by András Riedlmayer and the architect/architectural historian Andrew Herscher after the Kosovo war in 1999 the two developed a large database on the destruction of architectural heritage in Kosovo and mapped out the patterns of this devastation in order to provide evidence to the ICTY, where their report was presented numerous times.

26 Hito Steyerl, 'A Thing Like You and Me', *e-flux*, no. 15, April 2010.
Histories of violence are thus read out of the smallest fragments and singular objects 'penetrating ever more deeply into the inside of the object under scrutiny and *it describes a universe only within the object itself*.' Walter Benjamin, Section VI of *Moscow Diary*, Cambridge, MA: Harvard University Press, 1986.

27 Shoshana Felman and Dori Laub, *Testimony: Crises of Witnessing in Literature, Psychoanalysis and History*, London: Routledge, 1991. Annette Wieviorka, *The Era of the Witness, trans.*

Jared Stark, Cornell, NY: Cornell University Press, 2006. For both writers it was the Eichmann trial in Jerusalem that inaugurated the *era of testimony* in allowing witnesses for the first time to take central stage in the context of crimes against humanity and 'to write their own history'. Shoshana Felman, 'Theaters of Justice: Arendt in Jerusalem, the Eichmann Trial, and the Redefinition of Legal Meaning in the Wake of the Holocaust', *Critical Inquiry*, vol. 27, no. 2, Winter 2001: 201–38.

28 The South African Truth and Reconciliation Commission, the Australian National Inquiry into the Separation of Indigenous Children from their Families and Communities, and the Canadian Royal Commission on Aboriginal Peoples would be some of these examples. See also Rosanne Kennedy, Lynne Bell and Julia Emberley, eds., 'Decolonising Testimony: On the Possibilities and Limits of Witnessing', *Humanities Research*, vol. XV, no. 3, ANU E Press, 2009.

29 Robert L. Bernstein, 'Rights Watchdog, Lost in the Mideast,' *New York Times*, 19 October 2009.

30 Michal Givoni, 'Witnessing in Action, Ethics and Politics in a World Without Borders', from Adi Ophir, Michal Givoni and Sari Hanafi (eds), *The Power of Inclusive Exclusion*, New York: Zone Books, 2009.

31 Alain Badiou, *Ethics: An Essay on the Understanding of Evil*, trans. Peter Hallward, London: Verso, 2001; Rony Brauman, 'From Philanthropy to Humanitarianism: Remarks and an Interview', *The South Atlantic Quarterly*, vol. 103, no. 2/3, Spring/Summer 2004; Rony Brauman interviewed by Michel Feher and Philippe Mangeot, 'Learning from Dilemmas,' Michel Feher, ed., *Nongovernmental Politics*, New York: Zone Books, 2007. If for Agamben, Givoni and others, the camp was identified as the *par excellence* site in regards to which testimony is simultaneously both most relevant and most challenged, the mass grave has become the *par excellence* locus of forensics. Look out for the yet-unpublished Adam Rosenblatt, *Last Rights: International Forensic Investigations and the Claims of the Dead*, draft.

32 The increased UN mandate for human rights enforcement led the United Nations to create the Office of the High Commissioner for Human Rights (OHCHR) by a General Assembly resolution in 1993, and then in 2006 to establish the Human Rights Council. Since the inception of the first and increasingly since the establishment of the latter, 'objective', 'scientific' data were considered as useful to supplement the usual oral testimonies produced during the hearings.

33 Lorraine Daston and Peter Galison, *Objectivity,* New York: Zone Books, 2007.

34 The term 'material witness' was suggested by the spatial and cultural theorist Susan Schuppli in her account of the analogue materiality of media artefacts. Susan Schuppli, 'Of Mice, Moths and Men Machines', *Cosmos and History: The Journal of Natural and Social Philosophy*, vol. 4, no. 1–2, 2008.

35 The indicative pop culture example of this shift is the actor William Peterson. The first role for which he became famous was as the FBI agent Will Graham in Michael Mann's film *Manhunter* (1986), the first movie version of one of Thomas Harris's Hannibal Lecter novels. Peterson played an extreme case of the detective as psychologist – driven mad by his empathic capacity to put himself in the mind of a killer. His second role, however, was as Dr Gil Grisom, the main character in the original *CSI* (begun in 2000), where he was a borderline autistic and science geek, who hated dealing with people rather than objects.

36 Steve Goose, in HRW promotional video clip, online: youtube.com/user/Human RightsWatch#p/u/40/CDtDeXS-iuE

37 An HRW statement reads: 'Human Rights Watch maintains a position of neutrality on issues of *jus ad bellum* (law concerning acceptable justifications to the use of armed force), because it believes that it is the best way to promote our primary goal of encouraging all sides in armed conflicts to respect international humanitarian law, or *jus in bello* (law concerning acceptable conduct in war).'

38 This is what is referred to as 'the day after', with a rationale to leave an area sterile by razing it. 'That way', explained one of the Israeli soldier interviewees of Breaking the Silence, the organization of Israeli military veterans that exposes the realities of life in the Palestinian Occupied Territories, 'we have good firing capacity, good visibility for observation, we can see anything, we control a very large part of the area and very effectively.' See shovrimshtika.org/index_e.asp

39 Marc Garlasco interviewed by Eyal Weizman, New York City, 27 September 2009 (all other quotes from Garlasco are from this interview unless otherwise stated).

40 Please compare with Ariella Azoulay, 'The (In)human Spatial Condition: A Visual Essay', Adi Ophir, Michal Givoni and Sari Hanafi, eds., *The Power of Inclusive Exclusion: Anatomy of Israeli Rule in the Occupied Palestinian Territories*, New York: Zone Books, 2009.

41 Eyal Weizman, 'Lawfare in Gaza: Legislative Attack,' *Opendemocracy*, 1 March 2009.

42 Human Rights Watch, 'Precisely Wrong: Gaza Civilians Killed by Israeli Drone-Launched Missiles', 30 June 2009.

43 Josh White, 'The Man on Both Sides of Air War Debate', *Washington Post*, 13 Feb 2008.

44 Susanne Koelbl, 'The Pentagon Official Who Came in From the Cold', Spiegel Online, 4 March 2009. See also the documentary film by Charles H. Ferguson, *No End in Sight*. He was also featured in a *60 Minutes* story on US military targeting practices that aired 28 October 2007 on cbsnews.com/video/watch/?id=4402000n&tag=related;photo video

45 HRW, 'Leadership Failure: First hand Accounts of Torture of Iraqi Detainees by the US Army's 82nd Airborne Division', 22 September 2005, hrw.org.

46 NGO Monitor, 'Experts or Ideologues? HRW's Defense of Marc Garlasco's Nazi Fetish', 10 September 2009, ngo-monitor.org.

47 Garlasco did not hide his collection. He ascribed his fascination with Nazi-era memorabilia to his own family history: his maternal grandfather was a soldier in the Wehrmacht (his uniform was on display in a glass box in Garlasco's home). See John H. Richardson, 'Why Is This Good Man Getting Hung Out to Dry?', *Esquire*, 13 Oct 2009; and Marc Garlasco, 'Responding to Accusations', *Huffington Post*, 11 September 2009.

48 In his investigation of Israeli military actions in Gaza, Garlasco has also made some very serious errors. In June 2006, he found that an explosion on a Gaza beach that killed seven people had been caused by Israeli shelling. After meeting Israeli officers and being shown the result of an Israeli army investigation, he told the *Jerusalem Post* that he had been previously wrong, and that the deaths were probably caused by unexploded munitions in the sand. This admission was considered wrong by HRW, which did not accept Israeli explanations. Garlasco made his retraction in an HRW press release and he was reprimanded for uncritically accepting the Israeli version of events. For a contestation of the latter by NGO Monitor see 'Experts or Ideologues? The Gaza Beach Incident 2006', 8 September 2009, ngo-monitor.org

49 Bruno Latour, *On the Modern Cult of the Factish Gods*, Durham, NC: Duke University Press, 2010.

50 Hito Steyerl, 'A Thing Like You and Me'.

51 Aaron T. Wilson, 'Air Command and Staff College Air University Building the Perfect Beast: Proposals to Improve USAF Targeting Training', USAFR, April 2006.

52 Sina Najafi, Eyal Weizman and Eve Hinman, 'The Building Is Our Last Line of Defense: An Interview with Eve Hinman', *Cabinet*, issue 16, winter 2004/05.

53 Mark Benjamin, 'When Is an Accidental Civilian Death Not an Accident?', *Salon*, 30 July 2007.

54 Gregor Noll, 'Sacrificial Violence and Targeting in International Humanitarian Law', Ola Engdahl and Pål Wrange, eds., *Law at War: The Law as It Was and the Law as It Should Be*, Leiden: Martinus Nijhoff Publishers, 2008.

55 *60 Minutes*, 31 August 2008, CBS News.

56 'Off Target'. In this comprehensive 147-page report, HRW found that US forces could have prevented hundreds of civilian casualties by abandoning two faulty military tactics: the use of cluster munitions and heavy reliance on 'decapitation' strikes designed to kill Iraqi military and political leaders. The latter was the activity in which Garlasco was involved.

57 Jorella Andrews, *In-Situ: The Ethics of Standing and Staring*, forthcoming. In this work Andrews refers to 'the visual prolongation of a disastrous event'.

58 'Off Target', p. 20: 'Collateral damage assessments are a key way for the military to fulfil its obligations under international humanitarian law.'; 'For the most part, the collateral damage assessment process for the air war in Iraq worked well, especially with respect to pre-planned targets. Human Rights Watch's month-long investigation in Iraq found that, in most cases, aerial bombardment resulted in minimal adverse effects to the civilian population.'; p. 22: 'The aerial strikes on Iraqi leadership constituted one of the most disturbing aspects of the war in Iraq for several reasons… Many of the civilian casualties from the air war occurred during US attacks on senior Iraqi leadership officials.'

59 Interview, 27 September 2009.

60 Josh White, 'The Man on Both Sides of Air War Debate'.

Epilogue: The Destruction of Destruction

1 Peter Beaumont, 'Death and Devastation in Gaza Neatly Filed and Documented', *Guardian*, 29 May 2009. See also Kai Wiedenhöfer, *The Book of Destruction*, London: Steidl, 2011; and Peter Beaumont, 'Kai Wiedenhöfer's *The Book of Destruction*: Gaza: One year After the 2009 War', *Observer*, 23 January 2011.

2 Ariella Azoulay, 'The (In)human Spatial Condition: A Visual Essay', Adi Ophir, Michal Givoni and Sari Hanafi, eds, *The Power of Inclusive Exclusion: Anatomy of Israeli Rule in the Occupied Palestinian Territories*, New York: Zone Books, 2009.

3 Ibid.

4 Quoted in Emmanuel Sivan, 'The Lights of Netzarim' *Ha'aretz*, 7 November 2003.

5 Hanan Greenberg and Attila Somfalvi, 'Ashkenazi Hands Over Book of Targets to Gantz', Ynet, 14 February 2011.

6 Beaumont, 'Death and Devastation'.

7 W. G. Sebald, *On the Natural History of Destruction*, London: Hamish Hamilton, 2003.

8 Sharon Sliwinski, 'The Aesthetics of Human Rights', *Culture, Theory & Critique*, vol. 50, no. 1, 2009: 23–39.

 The first instance of a 'reconstruction' of the destruction of buildings (and people) in war that I have been able to trace centres on the destruction of the world-famous university library in the Belgian town of Louvain in 1914, which became a major propaganda issue, and came to be seen as the beginning of total war, a case of war crimes and war reparation. The original 'reconstruction' was by J. Bledier, who used captured soldiers' diaries to draw up the case. Alan Kremer, *Dynamic of Destruction: Culture and Mass Killing in the First World War*, Oxford: Oxford University Press, 2007.

9 Mahmoud Darwish, 'The House Murdered', trans. Fady Joudah. progressive.org/mag/darwishpoem.html

10 Imperial War Museum film archive. PAL 74 is an interview with Ivan Lloyd Phillips, Assistant District Commissioner and later District Commissioner of Gaza-Beersheba, who recalls ruins in Gaza in 1938. MGH 3619 from around 1938 includes snatches of scenes of damage.

11 'Reconstructing the Closure: Will Recent Changes to the Closure Policy Be Enough to Build in Gaza?', Gisha position paper, December 2010.

12 Walid Khalidi, *All That Remains: The Palestinian Villages Occupied and Depopulated by Israel in 1948*, Washington, DC: Institute for Palestine Studies, 2006.

13 In the twelfth century, in *Tahafut-ul-Tahafut* – a title that can be translated as 'the refutation of refutation' or indeed 'the destruction of destruction' – the Andalusian scholar ibn-Rushd (Averroes) critiques the Persian Sufiascetic Ghazali's *Tahafut-ul-Falasifa* (Destruction of Philosophers) in defence of classical philosophy, showing it is competent with the teaching of Islam.

14 Saree Makdisi, 'The Architecture of Erasure', *Critical Inquiry*, vol. 36, no. 3, Spring 2010: 519–59, 555–6.

15 Sandi Hilal, Alessandro Petti and Eyal Weizman, *Book of Return*, DAAR, September 2009. In this book – produced as a part of an installation and displayed in the context of our exhibitions in many institutions and biennales worldwide – we designed a cultural centre, a Finiq, in both Dheisheh Refugee Camp and on the ruins of the village of Miska destroyed in 1948. We write: 'Return is a political act that is continuously and incessantly practised at present and projecting an image into an uncertain future. It connects to a varied set of practices that we would like to call "present returns" thus grounding them in present day material realities. These practices necessitate the adoption of a stereoscopic vision that navigates the complex terrain between two places – the extraterritorial space of refuge and the out-of-bounds village of origin. Present returns must have simultaneous material effect in both the sites of origin and sites of displacement. The result might be a reciprocal extraterritoriality that connects these two sites.'

16 These scholars and architects, working sometimes privately and sometimes alongside UN agencies, have in different contexts attempted to challenge the conceptualization of refugee habitats as mere repositories of national memory. See Nasser Abourahme and Sandi Hillal, *The Production of Space, Political Subjectivication and the Folding of Polarity: The Case of Deheishe Camp, Palestine*, forthcoming; and Sari Hanafi, 'Palestinian Refugee Camps in Lebanon: Laboratories of State-in-the-Making, Discipline and Islamist Radicalism', TERRA, www.reseau-terra.eu/article798.html. For an interview with Ismael Sheikh Hassan, see: arteeast.org/pages/artenews/extra-territoriality/273

Index

when

    mr

        dog

            bites